PARABLE
AND
GOSPEL

PARABLE

AND

GOSPEL

Norman Perrin

Edited by K. C. Hanson

Fortress Press

Minneapolis

PARABLE AND GOSPEL
Fortress Classics in Biblical Studies

Cover image: *Wheat* by Thomas Hart Benton. Smithsonian American Art
Museum, Gift of Mr. and Mrs. James A. Mitchell and museum purchase. Used
by permission.

Author photo: Courtesy of the University of Chicago Divinity School. Used by
permission.

Library of Congress Cataloging-in-Publication Data

Perrin, Norman.
Parable and Gospel / Norman Perrin ; edited by K. C. Hanson.
      p. cm. — (Fortress classics in biblical studies)
Includes bibliographical references and index.
   ISBN 0-8006-3586-8 (pbk.)
1. Bible. N.T.—Criticism, interpretation, etc. 2. Bible.
N.T.—Theology. I. Hanson, K. C. (Kenneth C.) II. Title. III. Series.
   BS2361.3.P47 2003
   225.6—dc21
                            2002156638

Manufactured in the U.S.A.
08   07   06   05   04   03   1   2   3   4   5   6   7   8   9   20

Contents

Abbreviations

1QM	War Scroll (*Milḥamah*)
ABD	*Anchor Bible Dictionary*, ed. David Noel Freedman (1992)
AnBib	Analecta Biblica
BibIntSer	Biblical Interpretation Series
BibLim	Biblical Limits
BR	*Biblical Research*
BTB	*Biblical Theology Bulletin*
BZNW	Beihefte zur ZNW
CBNT	Coniectanea biblica: New Testament Series
CBQ	*Catholic Biblical Quarterly*
CBQMS	CBQ Monograph Series
ChrCen	*Christian Century*
DBI	*Dictionary of Biblical Interpretation*, ed. John H. Hayes (1999)
ESEC	Emory Studies in Early Christianity
FCBS	Fortress Classics in Biblical Studies
FRLANT	Forschungen zur Religion und Literatur des Alten und Neuen Testaments
FzB	Forschung zur Bibel
GBS	Guides to Biblical Scholarship
GPT	Growing Points in Theology
HTR	*Harvard Theological Review*
HTS	Harvard Theological Studies
IBT	Interpreting Biblical Texts
Int	*Interpretation*
IRT	Issues in Religion and Theology
JB	Jerusalem Bible

JBL	*Journal of Biblical Literature*
JBR	*Journal of Bible and Religion*
JR	*Journal of Religion*
JSNT	*Journal for the Study of the New Testament*
JSNTSup	JSNT Supplement Series
JTC	*Journal for Theology and the Church*
KEK	Kritisch-exegetischer Kommentar über das Neue Testament
LJS	Lives of Jesus Series
LTT	Library of Theological Translations
MMT	Makers of Modern Theology
MT	Masoretic text
NEB	New English Bible
NFT	New Frontiers in Theology
NovTSup	Novum Testamentum Supplements
NTL	New Testament Library
NTS	*New Testament Studies*
NTTS	New Testament Tools and Studies
NVBS	New Voices in Biblical Studies
PNTC	Pelican New Testament Commentaries
RelPer	Religious Perspectives
RSV	Revised Standard Version of the Bible
SABH	Studies in American Biblical Hermeneutics
SacPag	Sacra Pagina
SBL	Society of Biblical Literature
SBLDS	SBL Dissertation Series
SBLSP	*SBL Seminar Papers*
SBT	Studies in Biblical Theology
SemSt	Semeia Studies
SNTIW	Studies of the New Testament and Its World
SPNT	Studies in the Personalities of the New Testament
ThInq	Theological Inquiries
T.Mos.	*Testament of Moses*
TRu	*Theologische Rundschau*
USQR	*Union Seminary Quarterly Review*
VF	*Verkündigung und Forschung*
WUNT	Wissenschaftliche Untersuchungen zum Neuen Testament
ZNW	*Zeitschrift für die neutestamentliche Wissenschaft*
ZTK	*Zeitschrift für Theologie und Kirche*

Editor's Foreword

THE CAREER OF NORMAN PERRIN was a relatively brief one, but it spanned Britain, Germany, and the U.S. and dramatically affected the course of New Testament research. His brilliant investigations of the teachings of Jesus, literary criticism of the Gospels, New Testament theology, and hermeneutics continue to influence contemporary research.

Perrin was born to a working class family on November 29, 1920, in Wellingborough, Northamptonshire, England. World War II delayed the beginning of his university studies since he spent the war as an intelligence officer with the Royal Air Force in the Mediterranean. After the war, he completed his B.A. at the University of Manchester in 1949. At Manchester Perrin studied with T. W. Manson, a choice that remained influential throughout his career. Manson focused on the Son of Man traditions, the Kingdom of God, and penetrating the Jesus traditions to the earliest strata of his teaching. These all became important threads in the work of Perrin as well.

After Manchester, Perrin went on to London University, where he completed both the B.D. (1952) and M.Th. degrees (1955). During this time he served as pastor for Baptist congregations in London (Westbourne Park Baptist Church, 1949–52) and Swansea, South Wales (Sketty Baptist Church, 1952–56), having been ordained in 1949 in the Baptist Union of Great Britain and Northern Ireland.

Studying briefly in Berlin, Perrin's doctoral work at the University of Göttingen was directed by Joachim Jeremias. He benefited from Jeremias's use of the Hebrew Bible, Pseudepigrapha, Dead Sea Scrolls, and rabbinic materials in New Testament exegesis, as well as historical Jesus studies. Perrin's dissertation at Göttingen, "The Kingdom of God in the Teaching of Jesus" (1959), was revised and published in 1963. It traced the scholarly discussion on this topic from the early nineteenth century (Schleiermacher and Weiss) to the middle of the twentieth (Bultmann, Wilder, and Jeremias). Significantly, he dedicated the published edition to both Manson and Jeremias. Perrin was also influential in bringing Jeremias's work to English-speaking audiences by translating "The Problem of the Historical Jesus," "The Sermon on the Mount," and "The Lord's Prayer in Modern Research." (These are now available as chapters in Joachim Jeremias, *Jesus and the Message of the New Testament*, ed. K. C. Hanson, Fortress Classics in Biblical Studies [Fortress Press, 2002]).

Serendipitously, James M. Robinson, then at the Candler School of Theology at Emory University, was invited to be an external examiner for Perrin's dissertation. Robinson was influential in Perrin taking his first teaching position at Candler, where he taught from 1959 to 1964. Robinson's interest in New Testament theology, existentialist hermeneutics, and Gospel criticism provided Perrin with a dynamic discussion partner. From 1964 to 1976 Perrin taught at the Divinity School at the University of Chicago. Discussions with his Chicago colleagues Paul Ricoeur and Mircea Eliade influenced him significantly in his understanding of symbol, myth, and hermeneutics.

While Perrin is well-known for his use of redaction criticism—indeed one of his enduring works has been *What Is Redaction Criticism?* (Fortress Press, 1969)—one of his most important contributions was to promote the use of literary criticism in New Testament exegesis. He saw redaction criticism as only one part of that broader methodology. Certainly this concern has had a major impact on New Testament studies, and his literary sensitivities are clearly demonstrated in his innovative *The New Testament: An Introduction* (1st ed. 1974). That introduction has been revised three times by his former student, Dennis C. Duling (1982, 1994, and 2003).

Rudolf Bultmann's importance—exegetically and theologically—for Perrin was demonstrated in his volume *The Promise of Bultmann: The Promise of Theology* (Fortress Press, 1979; 1st ed. 1969). His debt to Bultmann was deep, and some of the key issues that Perrin drew on from Bultmann are form criticism and his sophisticated exegesis of the New Testament; concern for the relationship between the historical Jesus and the kerygma about Christ in the New Testament; the theological analysis of the New Testament; and existentialist hermeneutics. But he was also critical of Bultmann in several respects, notably: Bultmann's treatment of the Gospel writers as collectors of tradition rather than creative authors; Bultmann's emphasis on the theologies of Paul and John in his New Testament theology, while treating the Synoptic Gospels and the other books as having far less importance; and Bultmann's emphasis on the discontinuity between the historical Jesus and kerygmatic Christ to the detriment of significant continuities.

Perrin was still relatively young (56) when he died of heart failure in 1976, though he had battled with cancer since 1969. He was named President of the

Society of Biblical Literature in 1973, and he has received four tributes. The first was published as *Christology and a Modern Pilgrimage: A Discussion with Norman Perrin*, edited by Hans Dieter Betz (rev. ed., 1974), with assessments of his major contributions by New Testament colleagues. The second was an issue of *Journal of Religion* (64/4, 1984), with contributions by his former students and colleagues. Dennis C. Duling and M. Santiago created a video documentary, "Norman Perrin (1920–1976): A Tribute," which was presented at the annual meeting of the Society of Biblical Literature in 1996. And most recently, an issue of *Criterion* (37/1, 1998), a publication of the Divinity School at the University of Chicago, included tributes to him. For all these tributes, see the bibliography on pp. 139–40. The legacy of Perrin, however, is not only in his published works, but also his students. Besides a generation of seminarians in Atlanta and Chicago, he mentored doctoral students who became distinguished in New Testament studies, including John R. Donahue S.J. (emeritus, Jesuit School of Theology at Berkeley), Dennis C. Duling (Canisius College), Richard A. Edwards (Marquette University), Werner H. Kelber (Rice University), Vernon K. Robbins (Emory University), and Mary Ann Tolbert (Pacific School of Religion).

I have edited Perrin's essays in minor ways. Most importantly, endnotes have been added (marked by square brackets) as well as bibliographies in order to bring the reader up-to-date in the discussions. Headings have been added in a few places. A few minor changes have been made to make Perrin's language more consistently gender-inclusive in his earlier writings; this seems especially appropriate since he attempted to be inclusive in his later writings. I have also made occasional modifications in the RSV quotations by changing RSV's "LORD" to "Yahweh" and changing words such as "thou" to "you." The reader will also note that there are occasional overlaps between the chapters, which is due to their origin as independent essays.

I would like to express my gratitude to Nancy Perrin of Chicago, Illinois, for her permission to publish these articles. I also owe a debt of gratitude to my friend and colleague, Dennis Duling, for his advice and encouragement regarding this volume.

K. C. HANSON

Acknowledgments

The editor and the publisher are grateful to Nancy Perrin and the following journals for permission to publish these articles.

Chapter 1 was first published as "The Interpretation of a Biblical Symbol," *Journal of Religion* 55 (1975) 348–70.

Chapter 2 was first published as "Eschatology and Hermeneutics: Reflections on Method in the Interpretation of the New Testament," *Journal of Biblical Literature* 93 (1974) 3–14. Perrin delivered it as the Presidential Address at the Annual Meeting of the Society of Biblical Literature in Chicago, Illinois (November 9, 1973).

Chapter 3 was first published as "The Modern Interpretation of the Parables of Jesus and the Problem of Hermeneutics," *Interpretation* 25 (1971) 131–48.

Chapter 4 was first published as "The Evangelist as Author: Reflections on Method in the Study and Interpretation of the Synoptic Gospels and Acts," *Biblical Research* 17 (1972) 5–18.

Chapter 5 was first published as "The Interpretation of the Gospel of Mark," *Interpretation* 30 (1976) 115–24.

Chapter 6 was first published as "The Christology of Mark: A Study in Methodology," *Journal of Religion* 51 (1971) 173–87. It was reprinted in Perrin's *A Modern Pilgrimage in New Testament Christology* (Philadelphia, Fortress Press, 1974) 95–108, and in slightly revised form in William Telford, editor, *The Interpretation of Mark*, Issues in Religion and Theology 7 (Philadelphia: Fortress Press, 1985) 95–108.

Chapter 7 was first published as "Jesus and the Theology of the New Testament," *Journal of Religion* 64 (1984) 413–41.

Chapter 8 was first published as "The Challenge of New Testament Theology Today," *Criterion* 3 (1965) 25–34. Perrin delivered this as a "Fireside" presentation at the University of Chicago Divinity School (December 4, 1964).

The Kingdom of God—
Interpreting a Biblical Symbol

The purpose of this essay is to contribute to a general discussion of hermeneutics by focusing attention upon the history of the interpretation of one particular biblical symbol, the symbol Reign or Kingdom of God. My hope is that by means of a discussion of the ways in which this symbol has been interpreted we may throw some light on the interpretation of other biblical symbols and perhaps also on the interpretation of symbols in general. One advantage of discussing the symbol Reign or Kingdom of God is that it has a history of something like three millennia of use and reuse, of interpretation and reinterpretation, in the Bible and in the literature of the Judeo-Christian traditions. We have, therefore, a vast amount of data to choose from as we approach the subject, and I shall have to be highly selective in the periods, movements, and people I choose to discuss. I have tried to make the choice in terms of the contribution being made, directly or indirectly, to hermeneutical theory, but I am only too aware of the fact that the choices made are personal ones.[1]

THE ANCIENT NEAR EAST

The roots of the symbol Reign or Kingdom of God lie in the ancient Near Eastern myth of the Kingship of God. This "was taken over by the Israelites from the Canaanites, who had received it from the great kingdoms on the Euphrates and Tigris and Nile, where it had been developed as early as ancient Sumerian times."[2] In this myth the god had acted as king in creating the world, in the course of which he had overcome and slain the primeval monster. Further, the god continued to act as king by annually renewing the fertility of the earth, and he showed himself to be king of a particular people by sustaining them in their place in the world. This myth is common to all the peoples of the ancient Near East, and elements from one version of the myth were freely used in others. Essentially it is only the name of the god that changes as we move from people to people. In Babylonia Marduk is king; in Assyria, Asshur; in Ammon, Milcom; in Tyre, Melqart; in Israel, Yahweh.[3]

A feature of this myth of the Kingship of God was that it was celebrated annually in cultic ritual. In the ancient world, life was seen as a constant struggle between good and evil powers: the world was seen as the arena of this struggle. Each winter threatened to become a permanent blight on the fertility of the earth, and as each spring the god renews the fertility of the earth against the threat of his enemies and humanity's, each spring was a renewal of the primeval victory of the god over the monster. This was celebrated cultically in an annual New Year festival. In the cultic ritual of this festival the god became king as he reenacted the primeval victory of creation; he acted as king as he renewed the fertility of the earth; his people experienced him as king as he entered once more into their lives.

ANCIENT ISRAEL

That ancient Israel learned to think of their god in this way, and to celebrate his kingship in this way, can be seen from the so-called enthronement psalms (Psalms 47, 93, 96, 97, 98, 99) with their constant refrain, "Yahweh has become King!" a cultic avowal often mistranslated as "The LORD reigns."[4]

> Yahweh had become King; he is robed in majesty;
>   Yahweh is robed, he is girded with strength.
> Yea, the world is established; it shall not be moved;
>   your throne is established from of old;
>   you are from everlasting. (Ps 93:1-2)

> Yahweh has become King; let the earth rejoice;
>   let the many coastlands be glad!
> Clouds and the thick darkness are round about him;
>   righteousness and justice are the foundation of his throne.
>   (Ps 97:1-2)

> Say among the nations, "Yahweh has become King!
>   Yea, the world is established, it shall never be moved;
>   he will judge the peoples with equity." (Ps 96:10)

Already in the last two quotations we can see a characteristic Israelite emphasis being introduced into the myth: "righteousness and justice are the foundation of his throne" and "he will judge the peoples with equity" are reminiscent of the language of covenant traditions, and it is a reminder that major elements of Israelite theology were established among the Israelite tribes *before* they adopted the myth of the Kingship of God from their Canaanite neighbors. The adoption of the myth has to date from the period of the monarchy,[5] but already in the days of tribal confederacy (amphictyony) the (future) Israelite was confessing the salvation history:

> A wandering Aramean was my father; and he went down into Egypt and sojourned there, few in number; and there he became a nation, great, mighty, and populous. And the Egyptians treated us harshly, and afflicted us, and laid upon us hard bondage. Then we cried to Yahweh the God of our fathers, and Yahweh heard our voice, and saw our affliction, our toil, and our oppression; and Yahweh brought us out of Egypt with a mighty hand and an outstretched arm, with great terror, with signs and wonders; and he brought us into this place and gave us this land, a land flowing with milk and honey. And behold, now I bring the first of the fruit of the ground, which you, O Yahweh, have given me. (Deut 26:5b-10)

The conception of salvation history (*Heilsgeschichte*) is one introduced into the discussion of the theology of the Old Testament by Gerhard von Rad, who points out that in Deut 26:5b-9 we have what he calls a "credo," a confessional summary of the activity of God on behalf of his people.[6] Such credos are found elsewhere (for example, Deut 6:20-24, Josh 24:2b-13), and characteristically they dwell on the activity of God on behalf of his people in a sequence of events:

- Migrations of the Patriarchs and Promise of the Land (Canaan) to them
- Descent to Egypt and prosperity and oppression there
- Deliverance from Egypt at the Exodus
- Red Sea Miracle
- Wilderness Wandering
- Giving of the Land (Canaan, the land promised to the patriarchs).[7]

This constitutes the salvation history—the history of God's acts of salvation on behalf of his people—and it plays a major role in the development of ancient Israelite theology, as well as in the development of ancient Israelite literature, since it provides the basic structure for the Pentateuchal sources J, E, and P, and hence ultimately for the Pentateuch itself.

Therefore, the conception of a salvation history, and the practice of its confessional recitation at a festival at one or more of the amphictyonic sanctuaries, antedates the myth of God as King and its celebration in the temple at

Jerusalem, but the question of comparative dating is not important. What is important is that Israel inherited two traditions that concerned themselves in a very special way with the activity of God. One, the ancient Near Eastern myth, celebrated the activity of God in the act of creation and in the annual renewal of the world; the other, the amphictyonic *Heilsgeschichte*, celebrated the activity of God at crucial moments in the history of his people. It was natural and inevitable that these two should be brought together.

The two traditions are brought together in various ways. In the first place the enthronement psalms extend the act of the creation of the world by God to the act of creating and choosing his own people—that is, to include the fundamental thrust of the salvation history:

> Moses, Aaron were among his priests,
> > Samuel also was among those who called on his name.[8]
> > They cried to Yahweh, and he answered them.
> He spoke to them in the pillar of cloud;
> > They kept his testimonies, and the statutes that he gave them.
> > > (Ps 99:6-7)

Then, second, elements from the salvation history were interpreted in terms of characteristics of the creation myth. "The sea" where the Egyptians perished becomes the primeval sea (Exod 15:5, 8), Egypt is turned into "Rahab," the primeval dragon (Isa 30:7; 41:9; Ps 87:4; 89:11).[9] Finally, the two are brought together in literary units, as in Psalm 136.

> O give thanks to Yahweh, for he is good;
> O give thanks to the God of gods;
> O give thanks to the Lord of lords;
> To him who alone does great wonders,
> To him who by understanding made the heavens,
> To him who spread out the earth upon the water,
> To him who made the great lights,
> The sun to rule over the day,
> The moon and stars to rule over the night;
> To him who smote the first-born of Egypt,
> And brought Israel out from among them,
> With a strong hand and an outstretched arm;
> To him who divided the Red Sea in sunder,
> And made Israel pass through the midst of it,
> But overthrew Pharaoh and his host in the Red Sea;
> To him who led his people through the wilderness,
> To him who smote great kings,

And slew famous kings,
Sihon, king of the Amorites,
And Og, king of Bashan,
And gave their land as a heritage,
A heritage to Israel his servant;
It is he who remembered us in our low estate,
And rescued us from our foes,
He who gives food to all flesh;
O give thanks to the God of heaven.[10]

But the most obvious example of this process is the Pentateuch itself. At the time of the Solomonic enlightenment, the J document was written in Jerusalem: the J document is virtually a narrative account of creation and *Heilsgeschichte*. At the Exile, the P document followed this pattern, and it remained the pattern of the Pentateuch as we know it with the necessary changes introduced when the Deuteronomistic history was united with the creation plus salvation history narrative.[11] That this is an amalgam of two originally separate traditions can be seen rather dramatically in the fact that the E source of the Pentateuch does not include creation but begins directly with the Patriarchs.

With the bringing together of the two originally separate entities—the myth of God as King with its emphasis on creation and renewal and the myth of the salvation history with its emphasis on the activity of God on behalf of his people at key moments in their history—the stage was set for the emergence of the symbol Reign or Kingdom of God. At the level of language the symbol is derived from the myth of the Kingship of God, for *malkuth*, "Reign" or "Kingdom," is an abstract noun formed from the root *m-l-k*, "to reign, be king." At the level of immediate reference, however, the symbol evokes the features of the salvation history. What has happened is that the two myths came together to form one, the myth of God who created the world and is active on behalf of his people in the history of that world, and the symbol evolved to evoke that myth. I will quote two characteristic passages from the Old Testament to illustrate the meaning and use of Kingdom (of God) in the Old Testament.[12]

All your works shall give thanks to you, O Yahweh,
and all your saints shall bless you!
They shall speak of the glory of your kingdom,
and tell of your power,
to make known to the sons of men your mighty deeds,
and the glorious splendor of your kingdom.
Your kingdom is an everlasting kingdom,
and your dominion endures throughout all generations. (Ps 145:10-13a)

From this we can see that to speak of the "glory of [God's] kingdom" is to speak of "his might," of his "mighty deeds." Moreover, to say that the Kingdom of God is "an everlasting kingdom" is to say that God's "dominion endures throughout all generations." As a further definition of this, the psalm continues:

> Yahweh is faithful in all his words,
> > and gracious in all his deeds.
> Yahweh upholds all who are falling,
> > and raises up all who are bowed down. (Ps 145:13b-14)

In other words, to speak of the Reign or Kingdom of God is to speak of the mighty power of God, of his kingly activity, of the things he does in which it becomes manifest that he is indeed king.

Moving from the meaning of the symbol to that which it evokes, we turn to Exodus 15 and the Song of the Sea.[13] This concludes with the cry of exaltation, "Yahweh will reign for ever and ever" (15:18), and consists essentially of a recital of what are understood to be the mighty acts of God on behalf of his people, that is, the salvation history. He has delivered them from their captivity in Egypt and destroyed those who pursued them:

> Pharaoh's chariots and his host he cast into the sea;
> > and his picked officers are sunk in the Red Sea. (v. 4)

He has guided them through the wilderness and brought them to the Promised Land:

> You have led in your steadfast love
> the people whom you have redeemed,
> you have guided them by your strength
> to your holy abode. (v. 13)

Moreover, God has brought his people not only to the Promised Land but also to Mt. Zion, to Jerusalem and the temple that can now be established there:

> You will bring them in, and plant them on your own mountain,
> the place, O Yahweh, which you have made for your abode,
> the sanctuary, O Yahweh, which your hands have established. (v. 17)

In all this God was acting as king, and it is to be expected that he will continue to act as king on behalf of his people: "Yahweh will reign for ever and ever."[14]

In these early uses of the symbol we have a consistent myth, the myth of a god who had created the world and was continually active in that world on behalf of his people, with the emphasis upon the continuing activity of God. The symbol functions by evoking the myth, and in turn the myth is effective because it interprets the historical experience of the Israelite people in the world. They knew themselves as the people who had successfully escaped from Egypt, who had settled in Canaan, who had built the temple to their God on Mt. Zion. In their myth it was God who had done these things on their behalf, and by using the symbol in their songs of praise they evoke the myth and so celebrate their history as the people of God.

At this point it is obvious that I have begun to use the word "myth" in a particular way. It is a word that is notoriously difficult to define, but I like Alan Watts's statement, as quoted by Philip Wheelwright: "Myth is to be defined as a complex of stories—some no doubt fact, and some fantasy—which, for various reasons, human beings regard as demonstrations of the inner meaning of the universe and of human life."[15] A complex of stories—some no doubt fact, and some fantasy, that statement describes exactly the Israelite understanding of their deliverance from Egypt, their conquest of Canaan, the bringing of the Ark to Mt. Zion by David, and the building of the temple there by Solomon. "A complex of stories . . . which, for various reasons, human beings regard as demonstrations of the inner meaning of the universe and of human life." That, too, describes exactly the Israelite understanding of life in the world as being under the direct control of the God who had acted as king on their behalf *and who would continue to do so*. The ancient Israelite people believed that their myth of the kingly activity of God demonstrated "the inner meaning of the universe" and gave them a true understanding of the nature of human life in the world. It is because they believed this that the symbol was so effective: it was effective precisely because it evoked the myth by means of which they had come to understand themselves as the people of God, the beneficiaries of his kingly activity in the world. The symbol is dependent upon the myth, and it is effective because of its power to evoke the myth. The myth in turn derives its power from its ability to make sense of the life of the Israelite people in the world.

With this understanding of things, the historical destiny of the Israelite people in the world becomes an important factor in the functioning of the symbol and the effectiveness of the myth. So long as the people could celebrate their freedom as the people of God in the land God had given them they could celebrate his Reign or Kingdom in their temple, but in fact the freedom of the people of God in the land God had given them was a precarious historical phenomenon. Ancient Palestine was a buffer state between the two world powers centered on the fertile crescent of Mesopotamia to the north and on the Nile River to the south. Historically speaking, the ancient Israelite people were able to enter Canaan from the desert about 1100 B.C.E. because at that

time both the power to the north and the power to the south were comparatively ineffective. In Mesopotamia, Assyria was only just coming to power, and
in Egypt the so-called New Empire was in decline. This international situation
continued, so David was able to establish an independent Israelite state about
1000 B.C.E. But the situation did not continue indefinitely. In the north, Assyria
came to power and in the south Egypt revived, and Palestine became again a
buffer state between two world empires, its little independent kingdoms subject again to the control of the world powers. At the death of Solomon in 922
B.C.E. the Kingdom of Israel split in two, and the northern kingdom eventually
fell to an aggressive Assyrian king in 721 B.C.E. while the southern kingdom,
comparatively small and out of the way, managed to survive until 587 B.C.E.,
when it fell to a new power from the north, the Babylonians.

The details of all of this are of course unimportant in a discussion of the
interpretation of the biblical symbol, but what is important is the impact of
these historical events upon the use of the symbol Reign or Kingdom of God
with its evocation of the myth of God active as king on behalf of his people in
the world. To put the matter in a very summary form, what happened was that
prophets arose who interpreted these events in such a way that the myth
maintained its force. The catastrophes were the judgment of God upon his
people and their kings for not remaining true to him; the temporary reprieves
were signs that God was still active on behalf of his people. Above all, the
prophets used the ancient symbolism to express the hope for a new act of God
as King on behalf of his people, an act whereby he would deliver them from
their new captivity to Assyria or Babylon as once he had delivered them from
Egypt.

> For Yahweh is our judge, Yahweh is our ruler,
>   Yahweh is our king; he will save us. (Isa 33:22)

> How beautiful upon the mountains
>   are the feet of him who brings good tidings,
> who publishes peace, who brings good tidings of good,
>   who publishes salvation, who says to Zion, "Your God reigns." . . .
> Yahweh has bared his holy arm
>   before the eyes of all the nations;
> And all the ends of the earth
>   shall see the salvation of our God. (Isa 52:7, 10-11)

The most important element in the intricate historical process is perhaps
that this hope was in fact fulfilled. The Babylonians conquered Jerusalem and
exiled many of its people to Babylon in 587 B.C.E. Within fifty years, in 529

B.C.E., Cyrus, king of the Medes and Persians, conquered Babylon and took control of all the former Babylonian territories, including Syria and Palestine. Cyrus's policy was to allow people conquered and transported by the Babylonians to return home and rebuild their temples and sanctuaries, and within a year the Judeans had permission to return to Jerusalem and to rebuild their temple. Under these circumstances the Judean prophets were able to assert their myth and claim that Cyrus was in fact the servant of their God.

> Thus says Yahweh to his anointed, to Cyrus,
> > whose right hand I have grasped,
> > to subdue nations before him
> > and ungird the loins of kings,
> > to open doors before him that gates may not be closed:
> "I will go before you
> > and level the mountains,
> I will break in pieces the doors of bronze
> > and cut asunder the bars of iron,
> I will give you the treasures of darkness
> > and the hoards of secret places,
> that you may know that it is I, Yahweh,
> > the God of Israel, who call you by your name. (Isa 45:1-3)

Not only did the Judean prophets reassert the myth, they also returned to a use of the symbolism of the Reign or Kingdom of God.

> Sing aloud, O daughter of Zion;
> > shout, O Israel!
> Rejoice and exult with all your heart,
> > O daughter of Jerusalem.
> Yahweh has taken away the judgments against you,
> > and he has cast out your enemies.
> The King of Israel, Yahweh, is in your midst;
> > you shall fear evil no more. (Zeph 3:14-15)

"The King of Israel, Yahweh, is in your midst; you shall fear evil no more," thus exulted the prophet Zephaniah as the exiled Judeans returned to Jerusalem and began the tasks of rebuilding their temple and reconstructing the forms and expressions of their faith. Once again, however, the events of history called into question the validity of the myth. For two hundred years or so the Judean people lived quietly in Jerusalem and its environs as a theocracy ruled in the name of God by the high priest. But in 333 B.C.E. Alexander the Great conquered the Persian Empire. And, after his death and the establishment by his generals of their independent kingdoms, Palestine resumed its age-old status of an embattled buffer state between empires to the north and to the south—now Syria (ruled by the Seleucids) to the north and, as always, Egypt (now ruled by the Ptolemies) to the south. The days of virtual independence for a small Judean state centered on Jerusalem were over. Events resumed their ancient pattern: the Judeans were first under the control of the Ptolemies and then of the Seleucids.

Then there came a period of decline of both the Syrian and Egyptian powers, and the Judeans achieved independence again in 164 B.C.E. under Judas Maccabeus and his brothers. More than that, the successors of the Maccabeans were able to rebuild the Judean state to something like the size it had attained under David and Solomon. But this was due, as always, to the comparative decline of the world powers. Syria and Egypt were comparatively impotent, and Rome had not yet begun to exercise power in the eastern Mediterranean.

But in 63 B.C.E. this situation changed, and the Roman general Pompey appeared in Palestine to regulate the affairs of the eastern Mediterranean on behalf of Rome. Roman power was irresistible, and the Judean people again lost their independence as a result of a change in the international political situation.

After 63 B.C.E. the situation of the Judeans in Palestine was a particularly bitter one. They had returned from their captivity in Babylon exulting in God as King who had again delivered them. They had then known almost two centuries of virtual independence only to fall prey again to Egyptians and Syrians. Under Judas Maccabeus and his successors they had known another century of independence, and even a restoration of their state to something of its ancient glory. But now their situation was worse than ever. The Romans ruled in the land, and Jerusalem high priests, the representatives of God to the people and of the people before God, were appointed by Roman fiat. After 6 C.E. the situation worsened, for at that time the Romans began to rule Jerusalem directly through a Roman procurator.

Under these circumstances the Judean people continued to evoke the ancient myth, but now the formulations have a note of intensity about them, a note almost of despairing hope. In the *Testament of Moses,* an apocalyptic work written shortly before the time of Christ, we find the symbolic language of the Kingdom of God used as follows:

> And then his [God's] kingdom shall appear throughout his creation,
> and then Satan shall be no more,
> and sorrow shall depart with him . . .

For the Heavenly One will arise from his royal throne,
and he will go forth from his holy habitation
with indignation and wrath on account of his sons . . .
For the Most High will arise, the Eternal God alone,
and he will appear to punish the Gentiles . . .
Then you, O Israel, shall be happy . . .
and God will exalt you,
and he will cause you to approach the heaven of the stars.

(*T.Mos.* 10:1-9)

Here we have the symbolic language of the Kingdom of God being used again to express the hopes of the people. The myth remains the same—that of God as King active on behalf of his people—and the symbol remains the same—it is God's Kingdom that will appear—but the formulation has changed. On the one hand, the language has grown more metaphorical: "Satan shall be no more, and sorrow shall depart with him . . . the Heavenly One will arise from his royal throne . . . with indignation and wrath on account of his sons." On the other hand, the hope itself is coming to take a form in which the expectation is for a dramatic change in the circumstances of the Judeans over against the hated Gentiles. "The Most High will arise . . . he will appear to punish the Gentiles. . . . Then you, O Israel, shall be happy . . . God will exalt you . . . he will cause you to approach the heaven of the stars."

This is the language of apocalyptic, as this is the apocalyptic hope, and there is some question as to what the apocalyptic writers actually expected. It has been pointed out, above all perhaps by Amos Wilder, that apocalyptic imagery is a natural form of expression when one is in extreme circumstances; and Wilder himself has turned to it in poetry arising out of his combat experiences of the First World War.[16] What one can say perhaps is that the extremity of the situation of the Judeans under the Romans in Palestine after 63 B.C.E. escalated their use of language in the expression of the characteristic hope for the activity of God on their behalf, as it also created circumstances under which they were no longer sure what they hoped for—except that it was for a deliverance like those from Egypt and Palestine in the past, but this time a permanent deliverance from all the evils of history.

One particularly prominent form of this apocalyptic hope for a deliverance from history itself is that of the hope to begin a war against Rome in which God would intervene: a war that God would bring to an end by destroying the Gentiles and their Judean collaborators or sympathizers and creating a world transformed, a world in which "Satan and sin will be no more." Just how widespread and realistic this particular form of the apocalyptic hope was can be seen from the fact that the Judean people rose in revolt against Rome in 66 C.E.

and again in 132 C.E., both times beginning wars against Rome in which they expected God to intervene: wars that they expected God to bring to an end in victory for them as his people.

The people we have come to know through the Dead Sea Scrolls shared this hope. Indeed one of the Dead Sea Scrolls is a battle plan for this war against Rome and all evil, the war in which God would intervene and which he would bring to victory on their behalf. This is the so-called War Scroll (1QM), and in it we find a use of the symbolic language of the Kingdom of God. We read, "And to the God of Israel shall be the kingdom, and among his people will he display might," and "You, O God, resplendent in the glory of your kingdom . . . [are] in our midst as a perpetual help" (1QM 6.6 and 12.7). In both instances the symbol Kingdom of God is being used to express the hope—indeed the expectation—that God would act on behalf of his people by intervening in a war against Rome and the Roman legions. In this hope and expectation they began the war, but the war itself, contrary to their expectation, went the way of Rome and the Roman legions.

The symbol Kingdom of God is rooted in a myth concerning the activity of God as King on behalf of his people within history, and it is natural therefore that the understanding and use of the symbol should change in accordance with the historical experiences of the people using it. During the period of the control of Palestine by the Romans, the Jewish apocalyptic writers, despairing of history, turned to an expectation that God would bring to an end history as they knew it. But there is another way out of the dilemma posed by the intractability of actual historical experience—to shift the focus of expectation from the group to the individual. It is possible to think, on the one hand, of the historical experience of the people as a group, but it is also possible, on the other hand, to think of the experience of the individual in terms of the historicity of his or her existence in the world. This is the step taken by Jesus of Nazareth, and we turn now to a consideration of his use of the symbol of Kingdom of God.

JESUS AND THE KINGDOM

Jesus of Nazareth is, of course, a most important figure in Western religious and cultural history, and his life and teaching have been the object of sustained and intensive historical research ever since the rise of the modern historical sciences. Albert Schweitzer summarized and interpreted the research of the nineteenth century in a very widely read book, *The Quest of the Historical Jesus.*[17] The research of the twentieth century had not yet found its definitive interpreter, but one very notable feature of the most recent research, especially here in America, has been the attention given to Jesus' distinctive use of language, including the use of the symbolic language of the Kingdom of God.

Jesus proclaimed the Kingdom of God and in so doing used a symbol that had a rich history of use among the Israelite people, of use by prophets, priests, and apocalyptic seers. I have quoted some of those uses, and we have seen references to the deliverance of the Israelite people from Egypt, of their establishment in the Promised Land, and of the gift of the temple. We have read of the destruction of the Gentiles and of the people of God being exalted to the stars. But on the lips of Jesus we hear a rather different kind of language. We hear, for example, "The Kingdom of God is not coming with signs to be observed; nor will they say, 'Lo, here it is!' or 'There!' for behold, the Kingdom of God is in the midst of you" (Luke 17:20-21). Or again, "If it is by the finger of God that I cast out demons, then the Kingdom of God has come upon you" (Luke 11:20). Obviously I cannot now offer a detailed exegesis of these and other sayings of Jesus using the symbol Kingdom of God, but I can point out their remarkably personal nature. The Kingdom is *in the midst of you;* it is known in the restoration to wholeness of a shattered personality by means of an exorcism. In the proclamation of Jesus the Kingdom of God is related to the existential reality of the experience of individuals.

This is the conclusion I reached as a result of my own investigation of Jesus' proclamation of the Kingdom of God.[18] Now let me turn to the work of another scholar, John Dominic Crossan and his interpretation of the parables of Jesus,[19] specifically his interpretation of the Good Samaritan. The fundamentals of the parable as Jesus taught it are as follows:

> A man was going down from Jerusalem to Jericho, and he fell among robbers, who stripped him and beat him and departed, leaving him half dead. Now by chance a priest was going down that road; and when he saw him he passed by on the other side. So likewise a Levite . . . . But a Samaritan, as he journeyed, came to where he was; and when he saw him he had compassion . . . and took care of him. . . . (Luke 10:30-35)

The story ends with a deliberate challenge, "Which of these three, do you think, proved neighbor to the man who fell among the robbers?" and there is no doubt but that the story itself demands approval of the Samaritan. The dynamics of the story lead the hearer along the Jericho road, leave him lying in the ditch with the robbed man, hoping for help from the priest, from the Levite—in vain—and finding it finally at the hands of the Samaritan. The hearer applauds the Samaritan, is intended to applaud the Samaritan, and the "good Samaritan" has become a proverb in our Western culture. But the hearers of Jesus *despised* Samaritans. On both racial and religious grounds there was the deepest possible ill-will between Judeans and Samaritans. Yet the story demands that the Samaritan not be despised but rather approved. As

Crossan puts it, "When the story is read as one told to a Jewish audience by a Jewish Jesus, it is impossible to avoid facing the good man not just as good, but as Samaritan." The story itself demanded of those who first heard it that they conceive the inconceivable: "The whole thrust of the story demands that . . . [the hearer] say what cannot be said: Good + Samaritan."

Crossan speaks of moving from the literal point of the parable to its metaphorical point, and his conclusion is worth quoting in full:

> The literal point confronted the hearers with the necessity of saying the impossible and having their world turned upside down and radically questioned in its presuppositions. The metaphorical point is that *just so* does the Kingdom of God break abruptly into a person's consciousness and demand the overturn of prior values, closed options, set judgments, and established conclusions. . . . The hearer struggling with the contradictory dualism of Good / Samaritan is actually experiencing in and through this the in-breaking of the Kingdom. Not only does it happen like this, it happens in this.[20]

What is true of the parable of the Good Samaritan is true of other parables of Jesus. In the hands of Jesus the parable becomes a form of the proclamation of the Kingdom. As I put the matter at the conclusion of a discussion of a number of the parables in my *The New Testament: An Introduction*, "the hearers [of Jesus] are challenged to say what cannot be said, to applaud what should not be applauded, to recognize in the reversal of human judgments and human situations the sign of the breaking in of God's Kingdom."[21] It is in this way that the Kingdom comes.

The use of Kingdom of God by Jesus was, therefore, highly distinctive. The ancient Israelite concept of God active as king in the history of his people, at the level which in German could be called *Weltgeschichte* (world history), has been replaced by a concept of God active at the level of the historicity of the individual or the group (in German, *Geschichtlichkeit*).[22] But this distinctive use was not maintained in early Christianity. Indeed it was lost until it was recovered by modern scholarship in the twentieth century, a point to which we shall return below. Earliest Christianity did not, in fact, make extensive use of the symbol Reign or Kingdom of God; rather, it turned to other symbols by means of which it expressed its convictions concerning Jesus himself. In Bultmann's words: "the Proclaimer became the Proclaimed." The symbol was maintained, of course, because it was prominent in the Gospels and because the petition "Thy Kingdom come" was a constituent part of the Lord's Prayer. But this was due to the use by Jesus himself, and with the loss of the particular meaning given to the symbol by Jesus the symbol, as it were, "floated," becoming available for new uses and for new meanings to be given to it in Christian tradition.

AUGUSTINE AND THE KINGDOM

In the long centuries that separate the first century from the twentieth there are many uses of the symbol,[23] but we will concentrate on only one, the use by Augustine (354–430 C.E.), a major Christian theological figure. Augustine blended together what had become characteristically Christian ways of thinking with the rich heritage of Greek and Roman philosophy, and he did this when the Roman world was falling apart under barbarian onslaughts—Rome itself fell to Alaric the Hun in 410. We choose to discuss Augustine because he is the first major theologian to use the symbol reflectively or speculatively (and such a use by theologians continues into the present), and also because discussing him will give us the opportunity to introduce the views of Paul Ricoeur, whose book *The Symbolism of Evil* is a major contribution to the discussion of the interpretation of symbols in general and of biblical symbols in particular. We will begin with Ricoeur and with the context in which he himself mentions Augustine. Ricoeur is concerned with primordial symbols of stain, guilt, and defilement—symbols that are known and used almost universally—with "the fundamental symbols elaborated in the living experience of defilement, sin and guilt."[24] Having identified these symbols he goes on to observe that they are antecedent to the myths that explain and interpret them, such as the myth of the fall of humanity in the person of the primordial ancestor—the Adamic myth. The myth is "an interpretation, a hermeneutics, of the primordial symbols in which the prior consciousness of sin gave itself form."[25] The leitmotif of Ricoeur's interpretation of symbols is that "the symbol gives rise to thought." So, in this instance, the primordial symbols give rise to the Adamic myth. But the matter does not end there for there is a third level, a level reached as the symbols and their mythic interpretation give rise to speculation. We have a "second-degree rehandling" of the symbols and the myth in "the more intellectualized symbols of original sin."[26] Stated in summary form, Ricoeur's insight is that we must "distinguish three levels: first that of the primordial symbols of sin, then that of the Adamic myth, and finally the speculative cipher of original sin; and we shall understand the second as first-degree hermeneutics, the third as second-degree hermeneutics."[27] But we may distinguish three levels only if we start with the symbols themselves. Actually there is something prior to the symbols: there is "the living experience of defilement, sin and guilt" in which "the fundamental symbols [are] elaborated"; there is "the prior consciousness of sin" that "gave itself form" in the primordial symbols.[28]

In the discussion of primordial or archetypal symbols we may, therefore, distinguish four levels. First, the level of the consciousness or experience of humans that gives rise to or is expressed in the symbols. Then, second, the symbols themselves. Third, we have the myths by means of which the symbols are interpreted. Fourth, we may find the speculative reflection on the symbols and myths that further interprets them.

Assuming the first level, Ricoeur distinguishes the three further levels in connection with the symbolism of evil as follows: "first that of the primordial symbols of sin, then that of the Adamic myth, and finally the speculative cipher of original sin."[29] So we have the myth of the fall of primordial man, Adam, which interprets those symbols; then, further, we have speculation concerning original sin, which is secondary to the myth and tertiary to the symbols. In the context of our discussion it is important to note that Ricoeur recognizes that this speculative or reflective use of the symbols in Western thought is largely due to Augustine. This speculative use of the symbols is only, as he describes it, "a relationship of the second degree," and he deplores "the harm that has been done to souls, during the centuries of Christianity, first by the literal interpretation of the story of Adam, and then by the confusion of this myth, treated as history, with later speculations, *principally Augustinian*, about original sin. . . ."[30]

At the hands of Augustine the primordial symbols of sin, which had produced the myth of the fall of Adam, came to produce the speculative idea of original sin. Also at the hands of Augustine the myth of God active as king in the world on behalf of his people, which had produced the symbol of the Reign or Kingdom of God, came to produce the speculative idea of the Church as the Kingdom of God, and the Kingdom of God as the totality of redeemed humanity. Except that Augustine called this entity the City of God, the city of the saints:

> For the city of the saints is up above, although it produces citizens here below, and in their persons the City is on pilgrimage until the time of its kingdom comes. At that time it will assemble all those citizens as they rise again in their bodies; and then they will be given the promised kingdom, where with their Prince, they will reign, world without end. (*City of God* 15.1)

This Kingdom of God, this City of God, is, for Augustine, the church, not necessarily the Church as she is now, but as she will be at the end of time (for example, *City of God* 20.9). It was, of course, easy enough for the Church of the Middle Ages to take the next step and to equate the Kingdom of God with the hierarchical Church in the world, and the omnipotent Church became the Kingdom of God.

I do not have time to pursue these matters in any detail, but I would like to point out that in the use of the symbol Kingdom of God to represent the Church by Augustine and in the Middle Ages two very important facts are at work, one linguistic and one sociological. The linguistic factor has to do with the use of the symbolic language involved. In ancient Judaism, down to and including the proclamation of Jesus, the symbolic language is used *directly* in songs of praise, in exhortation, in the interpretation of events, or as the referent of stories like the Good Samaritan. The myth lies only one stage removed from the symbolic language, and the purpose of the language is directly to evoke the myth. But by the time of Augustine we have reached a culture dominated by allegory in which the symbol is not directly used but in which it is always represented by something else. If we take a characteristic passage from Augustine's *City of God,* we find him puzzling over the allegorical representation of the Kingdom of God in the texts of the New Testament:

> We must certainly rule out any reference to that Kingdom [i.e., the ultimate Kingdom of God] which he is to speak of at the end of the world, in the words, "Come you that have my Father's blessing, take possession of the kingdom prepared for you" [referring to Matt 25:34]; and so, even now, although in some other and far inferior way, his saints must be reigning with him, the saints to whom he says, "See, I am always with you, right up to the end of the world" [referring to Matt 28:20] for otherwise the Church could surely not be called his kingdom, or the kingdom of heaven. (*City of God* 20.9)

Here we can see that the symbolic language of the Kingdom of God is not being used directly but rather is being found represented in texts taken from the Gospels. The direct reference to the symbol, and the evocation of the myth by the symbol, is lost. Instead of evocation of the myth of the activity of God on behalf of his people we have reflection on the symbol indirectly represented in the text: we have room for speculation—in this instance speculation about the relationship between the Church and the Kingdom. The evocative power of the symbol is lost in the speculative reflection upon what are held to be indirect references to it in the text of the Gospels.

The second factor is the sociological factor of the change in the status of the community using the symbol. Israel was never an important state in the ancient Near East, and we have seen how difficult it was to maintain the use of the symbol Kingdom of God when the Israelite state was, historically speaking, usually under the control of more important powers, her destiny shaped by events over which she had no control. Moreover, Jesus and his followers were an insignificant group in Roman-controlled Palestine. And for the first three centuries of her existence, the Christian Church was a small, embattled sect in the Roman empire. But by the time of Augustine Christianity was the official religion of the empire, and after the fall of Rome in 410 the Church was the hope for civilization in the ruins of the empire. It is extremely interesting that precisely at this point the identification between the Church and the Kingdom of God begins to be made. The dramatic change in the sociological status of the community using the symbol has made possible an equally dramatic shift in the use of the symbol.

This all too brief discussion of Augustine, and Ricoeur, will have shown that Reign or Kingdom of God is a symbol of a different order or class than the symbols of guilt or sin, which are primordial or archetypal symbols. If we adopt Wheelwright's classification (see n. 28), then Reign or Kingdom of God is a "symbol of cultural range." But more important for our purpose is noticing the different function of myth in the case of the different symbols. In the case of the primordial symbols, the myth interprets the symbols and the consciousness or experience of humanity that the symbols evoke or elaborate. But in the case of the symbol Reign or Kingdom of God the myth is prior to the symbol, and the symbol is dependent upon it. The symbol evokes the myth, and when the myth becomes questionable or unacceptable then the use of the symbol changes, or the effectiveness of the symbol is lost. The symbol is effective only where the myth is held to be valid.

RAUSCHENBUSCH AND THE KINGDOM

The relationship between the validity of the myth and the effectiveness of the symbol is evident in the use of Kingdom of God in twentieth-century Christian tradition. In the twentieth century we can find a continuation of the direct use of the symbol to evoke the myth of God active in the world that we found to be characteristic of ancient Israelite poets and prophets. The most obvious name to quote here is that of Walter Rauschenbusch (1861–1918), who, in the period immediately before the First World War, deservedly came to be known as "the American prophet" and who was a leading force in the movement in American Christianity known as "the social gospel." Rauschenbusch deliberately made the symbol, the Kingdom of God, the central theme of his preaching and teaching.

Rauschenbusch was able to do this because he believed passionately in the ancient myth of a God active in the world on behalf of his people. The Kingdom of God, he proclaimed, is "the energy of God realizing itself in human life."[31] For him the ancient myth was a living reality, and it was for this reason that his use of the symbolic language of the Kingdom of God carried conviction. At the same time a social conditioning factor was also at work.

Rauschenbusch began his career by working as a Baptist minister in the noto-rious Hell's Kitchen area of New York City. And for eleven years he labored among people who, in the shadow of the world's greatest wealth, were "out of work, out of clothes, out of shoes, and out of hope." He was never to forget the endless procession of needy men and women who, as he put it, "wore down our threshold and wore away our hearts,"[32] and he came to see God as active precisely in the struggle to right their wrongs. He composed a litany for use in the Church, which in part reads as follows:

> From the corruption of the franchise, and of civil government,
> from greed and from the arbitrary love of power,
> Good Lord, deliver us.
> From the fear of unemployment and the evils of overwork,
> from the curse of child-labor and the ill-paid toil of women,
> Good Lord, deliver us.[33]

He saw God active as king precisely in that way.

The renewal of the ancient myth of God active as king in terms of the social struggle has been a major feature of recent American religious life, and it has brought with it a renewal of the use of the symbolic language of the Kingdom of God. A more recent example than that of Rauschenbusch has been called to my attention by one of my students, Kaci Creel, who tells me that one of the slogans under which Christian students took up the struggle for civil rights in the 1960s was "Go forth into the world and find out what in the world God is doing." The sense of riding with God on a bus as a "freedom rider" in the 1960s is a modern form of the ancient myth, and it made possible a renewal of the characteristic symbolic language.

BULTMANN AND THE KINGDOM

The direct use of the symbolic language of the Kingdom of God is made possi-ble by a renewal of the ancient myth. But what happens when the ancient myth becomes not only ancient but *archaic,* when it ceases to function as a demonstration "of the inner meaning of the universe and of human life"? This is a problem that plagues New Testament scholars because it is a fact that many of the New Testament myths have lost their power, and hence the sym-bolic language that evokes them has lost its force. The most ambitious attempt to meet this problem is that associated with the German New Testa-ment scholar, Rudolf Bultmann, who proposes to restore the force of the sym-bolic language by a sophisticated method of interpreting the myth, by a *hermeneutics.* The ancient myths, he says in effect, are attempts to describe the reality of life in the world, and therefore what we must do is to determine that aspect of the reality of life in the world being described by the myth and to redescribe it in nonmythological language. One of Bultmann's earliest attempts to do this is in connection with the use of Kingdom of God by Jesus, and on this he is worth quoting at some length.

> The Reign of God is a power that wholly determines the present, although in itself it is entirely future. It determines the present in that it forces man to decision: he becomes one thing or the other, chosen or rejected, his entire present existence wholly determined by it. . . . Jesus . . . sees man as standing in this crisis of decision before the activity of God. . . . If man stands in the crisis of decision . . . this is the essential characteristic of his being as a man.[34]

This is an attempt to translate the symbolic language of the Reign of God into the categories of an existentialist philosophy. It still maintains the language of the ancient myth in that it speaks of the "activity of God"; but on other occasions Bultmann made it quite clear that he was fully prepared to translate that language also. For Bultmann the activity of God is to be seen precisely in those aspects of life that force a person to decision; and the supreme gift of God is the ability to make the decision that leads to authentic existence in the world.

This interpretation of Kingdom of God in the message of Jesus was originally published in 1926, but it bears all the hallmarks of his famous "demythologizing" program, formally announced twenty years later.[35] This program remains perhaps the most important contribution to the general discussion of hermeneutics by a New Testament scholar, and it is too well known to need further discussion here.[36] There are some things, however, that must be said about Bultmann's interpretation of the symbol Kingdom of God in the message of Jesus and, perhaps by implication, about his demythologizing program.

In the first place, Bultmann has succeeded, by his sophisticated hermeneutics, in recapturing major emphases from Jesus' use of the symbol. Since his concern was to interpret Kingdom of God as used by Jesus this must be counted a gain for his hermeneutical method. It remains a question, however, whether that gain could not be achieved by other means.[37] A second, and much more important, point to be raised is the question as to whether we should abandon myth to an existentialist interpretation of human existence in the world, as Bultmann does. We have seen that the biblical symbol functions only in the context of the acceptance of a myth, and today there are problems with the acceptance of the biblical myths. Bultmann saw this problem clearly—and dealt with it somewhat drastically! But in this context there also remains a question, namely, the question as to whether myths are quite as monolithic as Bultmann sees them. Some are susceptible to, and indeed even demand, the existentialist interpretation Bultmann gives them, but others may perhaps require a different approach. The nature and function of myths and their proper interpretation in a world in which they no longer function as naturally as they did in the world in which the biblical symbols were created—these are clearly questions for further discussion.

A third point to be raised is nonetheless important for being very obvious. That is, we cannot discuss the interpretation of a biblical symbol without recognizing that *as a symbol* it has features in common with other biblical and nonbiblical symbols and that it therefore cries out for investigation in the context of a consideration of symbols in general. It is in this context that works such as Ricoeur's *The Symbolism of Evil* and Wheelwright's *Metaphor and Reality* become important to the interpretation of a biblical symbol (see chapter 2).

CONCLUSION

I am aware of the fact that in this essay I have not succeeded in developing a hermeneutics of a biblical symbol, but I may perhaps have identified some questions for further discussion. I have sought to establish the fact that the biblical symbol Reign or Kingdom of God functions in the context of the acceptance of the myth of God active as king in the world on behalf of his people. This myth itself, I have argued, is an amalgam of two earlier myths, the ancient Near Eastern myth of Kingship of God and the specifically Israelite myth of salvation history. Once established, the symbol depended for its effectiveness in part upon the historical experience of the people using the symbol. When that historical experience was such as to question the validity of the myth that the symbol served to evoke, then the frame of reference tended to change, either to a transhistorical reference, as in the case of apocalyptic, or to a framework of personal historicity, as in the proclamation of Jesus. Social factors could also influence the use of the symbol in other ways, as the change in the social status of the Church influenced the use of the symbol by Augustine, and the use of the symbol could also be affected by changes in the understanding of the nature of the text and language in which the symbol was expressed, as was also the case for Augustine. I then argued that in the twentieth century we have seen a resurgence of the direct, one might almost say classical, use of the symbol on the part of the people for whom the myth is once more a living reality and the development of a specific hermeneutics for the interpretation of the symbol on the part of a scholarship for which that is no longer the case. This led me to attempt a definition of our present task so

far as the hermeneutics of biblical symbols is concerned: a further consideration of the nature, function, and proper interpretation of the myths upon
which the symbols depend and which they serve to evoke, and a further investigation of biblical symbols in the context of the investigation of symbols in
general.

2

Eschatology and Hermeneutics

A feature of New Testament scholarship at the moment is that, as is the case with all academic disciplines, we are witnessing a veritable explosion of information. We have had extremely important discoveries, for example, the Qumran texts and the Nag Hammadi codices. And we have had equally important methodological developments, for example, the rise of redaction criticism. At the same time, our fundamental concern, hermeneutics, has become a focal point of concern for scholars from disciplines other than those of theological or biblical scholarship. Here I need only mention in German, Hans-Georg Gadamer, *Wahrheit und Methode* (1960; ET: *Truth and Method*, 1975); in French, Paul Ricoeur, *Le conflit des interpretations* (1969; ET: *Conflict in Interpretations,* 1974); in Italian, Emilio Betti, *Teoria generale della interpretazione* (1955), and in English, E. D. Hirsch, *Validity in Interpretation* (1967) to show that we are in the midst of a very lively multilingual and interdisciplinary debate.[1]

In view of these developments I want to take this opportunity to address myself in general terms to the question of method in the interpretation of the New Testament. At the same time, I am almost constitutionally incapable of discussing anything "in general terms." I much prefer to take a concrete example and then to reflect more generally in light of it. The natural example for me to take in this instance is eschatology, for this has been a constant concern of mine throughout the years. But eschatology is itself a very broad subject, so I shall focus attention quite concretely upon one particular form of it, that is, "Kingdom of God" in the proclamation of Jesus.

The advantage of focusing attention concretely on this form of eschatology for me is, of course, that it is a subject with which I can claim a degree of familiarity. I began my academic career with a doctoral dissertation directed towards it.[2] And when I was invited to present a paper to a seminar we held last year in Los Angeles I returned to it.[3] But there is another point, more important than my familiarity with the subject, and that is that in a consideration of the Kingdom of God in the proclamation of Jesus the methodological issues come very sharply into focus. Today these issues are my primary concern.

In any discussion of the Kingdom of God in the teaching of Jesus the first methodological issue to come into focus is *the importance of historical criticism*. By "historical criticism" I mean that aspect of our scholarly endeavor by means of which we seek to determine what "Kingdom of God" was intended to mean in the proclamation of Jesus, what the teaching concerning this subject was intended to say. To put the matter in the language of a more general discussion of hermeneutics, "historical criticism" describes the attempt to understand the meaning of a text in its specific and original historical context, the endeavor to recover, so far as is possible, the meaning intended by the author and understood by the first readers or hearers.

The modern historical-critical discussion of the Kingdom of God in the proclamation of Jesus may be said to have begun in 1892 with the publication of Johannes Weiss's *Die Predigt Jesu vom Reiche Gottes* (ET: *Jesus' Proclamation of the Kingdom of God*, 1971).[4] Weiss claimed that in the proclamation of Jesus the Kingdom of God was an overpowering divine storm that erupted into history to destroy and to renew, a storm that humans can neither bring about nor prevent. Moreover, Weiss further claimed that Jesus had proclaimed the outbreaking of this divine storm as imminent, but nonetheless as future. In other words, he interpreted Kingdom of God as an apocalyptic concept in the teaching of Jesus and then interpreted that teaching as claiming that the coming of the apocalyptic Kingdom was an event to be anticipated in the immediate future. We are all aware of Albert Schweitzer's popularization of this understanding and of the violent debate it occasioned, a debate that is as yet unresolved.[5]

From the standpoint of *method* the historical-critical work begun by Weiss and continuing to this day on the Kingdom of God in the teaching of Jesus is simply characteristic of historical criticism altogether. One seeks to establish the cultural-historical milieu of the message of Jesus and to come to understand that milieu using all the resources of historical scholarship, including finally an act of historical imagination. One seeks to establish the actual text of the teaching of Jesus from the sources available to us and then to understand that teaching in terms of its historical context. Put that way, it sounds simple; and indeed from the standpoint of methodological theory, it is simple. Although, as we are all only too well aware, in practice it turns out to be inordinately complex, as indeed does all historical-critical work on texts from another time and another culture. But the theoretical principles involved in historical criticism are thoroughly established and well understood, and I need spend no time discussing them. Instead I turn immediately to what is neither thoroughly established nor well understood, and that is the relationship between historical criticism and hermeneutics.

Now I need to define my terms again and say what I mean by "hermeneutics." Here I am content to follow Wilhelm Dilthey and Rudolf Bultmann and to define hermeneutics as "the art of understanding expressions of life fixed in writing."[6] There is, however, one point that I must emphasize since it is really the crucial point and that is what is meant by "understanding" when one speaks of an "expression of life" being "understood." Those of us who stand in the hermeneutical tradition epitomized by such names as Schleiermacher, Dilthey, and Bultmann would insist that "understanding" must be interpreted broadly and deliberately to include a conscious concern for relevance to and impact upon the interpreter and the interpreter's life. For those of us for whom texts are, in Dilthey's phrase, "expressions of life fixed in writing," the model of the relationship between the interpreter and the text being interpreted is that of meaningful dialogue.

The relationship between historical criticism and hermeneutics is, then, in my view, that of a first and a second stage of the total process of coming to understand a text and of entering into meaningful dialogue with it. In the case of texts from the past or from a different culture the task of historical criticism can be both difficult and quite inordinately complex, but in the case of any text it is essential. I would never accept a view of hermeneutics that did not see historical criticism as the essential first step in coming to understand any text, whether from the ancient past or today's newspaper. At the same time, historical criticism is only the beginning of the process of coming to understand a text, not its end.

Historical criticism is essential to hermeneutics, but it is not in and of itself hermeneutics. Essential to the process of understanding is the further step of meaningful dialogue with the text in terms of relevance and impact. This I hold to be true not only in the case of religious texts but of any texts that are "expressions of life fixed in writing." It is true of the rock musical *Hair* every bit as much as of *Godspell*. It is, I hope, clear that I am using the word "text" only as one form of the "expression of life." What I have said of written texts would apply equally to oral texts and, by the same token, to any form of human artistic expression.[7]

To return to Johannes Weiss and his interpretation of "Jesus' proclamation of the Kingdom of God," one most interesting aspect of his work was that he became convinced of the validity of his historical-critical understanding of Jesus' proclamation, but that he then could see little relevance of this understanding for him or the theology of his day. The apocalyptic eschatology of Jesus could be understood historically, but it had little hermeneutical significance for a theologian of the late nineteenth century. The editors and translators of Weiss's book, Richard H. Hiers and David L. Holland, make this point very perceptively in their introduction. Weiss, they say, "articulated an issue which went beyond the historical question of Jesus' eschatology, namely, the question of the relation of the results of historical scholarship and contemporary theology . . . he raises the question of hermeneutics."[8] Having raised this question, Weiss was almost entirely negative in his response to it. He wanted to keep his contemporaries honest and to make them refrain from imputing their conception of the Kingdom of God to Jesus; but in the end it was the late nineteenth-century understanding of the Kingdom of God that Weiss himself was prepared to accept and not that of Jesus. He could and did argue that "Jesus did not use the term 'Kingdom of God' to refer to the 'supreme ethical ideal,'" but then he could go on and define "Kingdom of God" for a contemporary theological understanding as "the *Rule* of God [that] is the highest Good and the supreme ethical ideal," freely admitting that "this conception of ours of the *basileia tou theou* [Kingdom of God] parts company with Jesus' at the most decisive point."[9]

It is very important in the context of a discussion of hermeneutics to recognize why Weiss could arrive at the historical understanding of the Kingdom of God in the proclamation of Jesus as essentially an apocalyptic concept concerned with an overwhelming divine storm that would erupt into history to destroy and renew, but nonetheless could himself continue to think in terms of the rule of God, which is the highest good and the supreme ethical ideal. It is not enough to say simply that he reached the conclusion that his historical understanding of Kingdom of God in the teaching of Jesus had little relevance for his own personal theology or his own religious life. The question is: Why did he reach this conclusion? That question is no sooner asked than answered, for the answer is quite clearly "because of his presuppositions," or, if you like, "because of the element of cultural conditioning in any act of interpretation." Weiss, himself both a product of a vital part of the late nineteenth-century German liberal theological movement, could appreciate *historically* an apocalyptic eschatology in the message of Jesus, but *existentially* he was too committed to "the highest Good" and "the supreme ethical ideal" as the essence of the religious life to find in that historical understanding any direct challenge to his own theology and his personal religious life.

If the modern historical-critical discussion of Kingdom of God in the teaching of Jesus may be said to have begun with Johannes Weiss, then it may certainly be further said that the single most important contributor to that discussion is Weiss's pupil, Rudolf Bultmann. Bultmann is such a towering figure in biblical and theological studies, and his work has been so widely and thoroughly discussed, that I need spend no time on this occasion in a general description of his work but turn immediately to his discussion of Kingdom of God in the proclamation of Jesus.

Bultmann begins by accepting his teacher Weiss's contention that Jesus' conception of Kingdom of God was essentially that of ancient Jewish apocalyptic. In his *Primitive Christianity in Its Contemporary Setting* he writes of "the eschatological preaching of Jesus" and describes it as "controlled by an imminent expectation of the Reign of God," affirming that in this Jesus "stands in line with Jewish eschatology in general. . . ."[10] At the same time he has reservations about this.

> If Jesus takes over the apocalyptic view of the future, he does so with considerable reductions. The unique feature of his teaching is the assurance with which he proclaims that *NOW* the time has come. The Reign of God is breaking in. The time of the End is at hand.[11]

Historically speaking, Jesus was mistaken. "Of course," says Bultmann, "Jesus was mistaken in thinking that the world was destined soon to come to an end." But although he was mistaken in the form of his expectation—that God was about to bring the world to an end—there is still validity in Jesus' proclamation because that proclamation expresses Jesus' *understanding of life,* and the understanding of human life implied by the proclamation of Jesus concerning the Kingdom of God "clearly does not stand or fall with his expectation of the end of the world." Jesus' expectation of the end of the world, with its concomitant expectation of the judgment of the world, is important as an indication of the fact that Jesus sees the world "exclusively *sub specie Dei* [from God's vantage point]."[12]

In his famous essay "The Problem of Hermeneutics," Bultmann specifically accepted Dilthey's definition of hermeneutics as "expressions of life fixed in writing"; and in his discussion of the eschatology of Jesus we can see the importance of his acceptance of Dilthey's understanding of a text as an "expression of life." For Bultmann, Jesus' proclamation of the Kingdom of God is an expression of Jesus' "understanding of life," of his "understanding of existence," of his "self-understanding." We could go so far as to say that it is an expression of Jesus' "vision of reality" and still be formulating Bultmann's conception. For Bultmann, Jesus' proclamation is a text to be interpreted, and, as a text, it is an "expression of life."

Bultmann's understanding of the nature of Jesus' proclamation of the Kingdom as a text enables him to look beyond the paraphernalia of the Son of Man coming on the clouds of heaven to bring the world to an end, and so on, to the meaning of this apocalyptic mythology as an "expression of life." As an expression of life the proclamation of Jesus means that Jesus sees the world as from God's vantage point (*sub specie Dei*); it means that Jesus sees humans as confronted by the immediacy of God and being challenged to decision. It is because he sees the proclamation of Jesus in this way that Bultmann can describe that proclamation as he does in his book *Jesus and the Word:*

> The Reign of God is a power which wholly determines the present although in itself it is entirely future. It determines the present in that it forces man to decision. . . . Because Jesus so sees man as standing in the crisis of decision before the activity of God, it is understandable that in him the Jewish expectation becomes the absolute certainty that now the hour of the breaking-in of the Reign of God has come. If man stands in the crisis of decision then . . . it is understandable that for Jesus the whole contemporary mythology should be pressed into the service of this conception of human existence.[13]

When I first translated and commented on this passage, I simply did not understand it. All I could think to say was: "It is difficult to see how far Bultmann regards Jesus as the author of this existentialist understanding of eschatology."[14] I can only thank those who must have known better for their forbearance in not publicly taking me to task for my lack of understanding of the Bultmannian hermeneutic, and now I hasten to correct myself. Bultmann can and does regard Jesus as the author of this understanding of eschatology because he sees it as a valid interpretation of the "understanding of life" that is being expressed in the apocalyptic mythology that Jesus in fact used.

Bultmann's interpretation of the eschatology of Jesus is very important indeed from the standpoint of method. What he has done, in effect, is to offer a solution to the problem of the relationship between historical criticism and hermeneutics. By means of historical criticism he establishes that Jesus made use of ancient Jewish apocalyptic mythology in his proclamation, with the significant difference that there was an element of immediacy in that proclamation that was lacking in other ancient Jewish apocalyptic. At that point Bultmann's understanding of hermeneutics takes over. He views the oral text of this apocalyptic proclamation as an expression of Jesus' understanding of life. Now two things become important. In the first place, it no longer matters whether Jesus was mistaken or not about the coming end of the world. What is important is not the accuracy of Jesus' expectation concerning the future of the world but the validity of his understanding of life in the world. Then, secondly, Bultmann has found a way of bridging the gap between the ancient Jewish apocalyptic preacher and the modern interpreter: both are concerned to come to an understanding of life in the world and hence meaningful dialogue can take place between them.

Bultmann's achievement in interpreting the eschatology of Jesus is breathtaking; neither the interpretation of the Kingdom of God in the proclamation of Jesus nor the understanding of hermeneutics among New Testament scholars was ever to be the same again. He himself was, of course, to go on to elaborate his hermeneutical method further in his demythologizing program. But I need not go into that program and the controversy it aroused because my concern is specifically with the discussion of the eschatology of Jesus as a means of approaching the problem of hermeneutics. I will, therefore, stay with Bultmann's interpretation of the eschatology of Jesus, and since I have already acknowledged my admiration for it as a breathtaking achievement I may now go on to raise some questions with regard to it.

The first such question to be raised is in connection with Bultmann's historical-critical understanding of the proclamation of Jesus: Is it valid, or has subsequent research invalidated it in any serious manner? The answer to this question has to be that by and large it is still valid. Jesus did proclaim a message couched in the imagery of ancient Jewish apocalyptic; and yet, at the same time, there are some significant differences between Jesus and other ancient Jewish apocalypticists. I myself would want to argue the point that Jesus did not in fact use the particular imagery associated with the Son of Man of Dan 7:13; but that is a comparatively minor difference. Jesus certainly did use the imagery associated with "Kingdom of God," and he did use it with an intensity and a sense of immediacy that distinguishes his message from that of other apocalyptic preachers of his generation in ancient Israel. Bultmann established that point and subsequent intensive research has not shaken it, and that is really the point at issue. I myself want to expand beyond Bultmann somewhat in connection with the difference between Jesus and the other apocalyptic preachers of his generation in ancient Israel, but only in the sense of building upon the foundations Bultmann has laid. But before I do that I must introduce a third category into this discussion. Having said something about historical criticism and hermeneutics, I now wish to turn to a third category, literary criticism.

Many New Testament scholars, and indeed many textbooks in New Testament studies, tend to think of literary criticism as concerned with such questions as authorship, date, and sources of the New Testament documents. This is, indeed, a legitimate use of the term, but literary criticism does in fact go beyond this and discusses also issues as those of the function of specific literary forms and of distinct kinds of language. Let me give some examples of what I mean.

In Paul's letter to the Philippians we would recognize that in 2:5-11 the apostle is quoting a christological hymn. That is a form-critical and literary-critical question. But under the rubric of literary criticism we must also ask: What difference does it make that Paul here quotes a hymn rather than indulging in a flight of rhetoric (which, incidentally, he was quite capable of doing)? What does a hymn do in terms of evoking a response from the reader that a flight of rhetoric from a master preacher would not do?[15]

To take another example, as my published work indicates, I have been particularly impressed by Ernst Käsemann's work on what he calls "sentences of holy law" (*Sätze heiligen Rechtes*) in the New Testament.[16] True, I would much prefer to call them "eschatological judgment pronouncements," because that is what they are; but there is no doubt but that Käsemann has identified both a literary form—a pronouncement of eschatological judgment upon dissident members of early Christian congregations—and its setting in life—the early Christian Eucharist. Accepting this, I want to go on to ask the question: Why then do we find this form in places where a eucharistic context is out of the question, for example in Mark 8:38 or Matt 6:14-15? It must be that the author of these texts in their present contexts expected them to have a particular force, and to function in a particular way, a force or function that another literary form would not have to do in that context. An eschatological judgment pronouncement was expected to evoke a particular kind of response that another literary form would not evoke and hence it was used in preference to another literary form, however unconsciously on the part of the author. Incidentally, may I venture the aside that I say "however unconsciously on the part of the author" only to avoid cluttering up the discussion of eschatology and hermeneutics by introducing the question of how far and in what ways the New Testament writers were in fact literary *authors*. In our present context any such discussion is irrelevant. What is relevant is the fact that an eschatological judgment pronouncement *functioned* in a way that another literary form would not have functioned: it evoked a response on the part of the reader or hearer that another form would not have evoked.

I want, therefore, to define literary criticism so as to include consideration of the ways in which literary forms and types of language *function*, and a consideration of the nature of *response* they evoke from the reader or hearer.[17] It can be seen that for me there is a close relationship between literary criticism and hermeneutics because if a consideration of literary form and type of language is literary criticism, then a consideration of their function, especially of the nature of the response they evoke, is hermeneutics. Now let us return to the discussion of Kingdom of God in the proclamation of Jesus in light of this understanding of literary criticism and its relationship to hermeneutics.

At the 1972 Society of Biblical Literature meeting in Los Angeles I argued that a hitherto unduly neglected factor in the discussion of the eschatology is the literary-critical fact that "Kingdom of God" is a *symbol*.[18] True, it is an ancient Jewish *apocalyptic* symbol, but it is nonetheless a *symbol*. I want to return to that point now because it seems to me that to consider the nature and function of Kingdom of God as a symbol is one way of making progress beyond Bultmann in the discussion of the eschatology of Jesus. Let me, therefore, now return in a rather different context to some of the things I discussed last year.

My understanding of the nature and function of symbol is heavily influenced by Philip Wheelwright, *Metaphor and Reality*, and Paul Ricoeur, *The Symbolism of Evil*. I begin, therefore, with Wheelwright's definition of symbol: "A symbol, in general, is a relatively stable and repeatable element of perceptual experience, standing for some larger meaning or set of meanings which cannot be given, or not fully given, in perceptual experience itself."[19] A symbol therefore represents something else, and Wheelwright makes a most important distinction within symbols in terms of their relationship to that which they represent. A symbol can have a one-to-one relationship with that which it represents, such as the mathematical symbol π (*pi*), in which case it is, in Wheelwright's terms, a "steno-symbol." Or it can have a set of meanings that can neither be exhausted nor adequately expressed by any one referent, in which case it is a "tensive symbol."

Paul Ricoeur makes a similar distinction. For Ricoeur a symbol is a sign, something that points beyond itself to something else. Not all signs are symbols, however, for sometimes a sign is transparent of meaning and is exhausted by its "first or literal intentionality." But in the case of a symbol the meaning is opaque and we have to erect a second intentionality upon the first, an intentionality that proceeds by analogy to ever deeper meanings. Concerned with the symbolism of evil, Ricoeur discusses "defilement." This is a sign in that it has a first, literal intentionality; it points beyond itself to "stain" or "unclean." But "defilement" is also a symbol because we can, by analogy, go further to a "certain situation of man in the sacred which is precisely that of being defiled, impure."[20] What for Wheelwright is a distinction between a steno-symbol and a tensive symbol is for Ricoeur a distinction between a "sign" and a "symbol."

These distinctions are modern distinctions, but they are distinctions in the way people use language and as such they are applicable to the use of language by any person at any time. It is my claim now that these distinctions are applicable to the proclamation by Jesus of the apocalyptic symbol "Kingdom of God," and that this literary-critical distinction is important at the level of both historical criticism and hermeneutics.

Let me begin this aspect of my discussion by pointing out that in ancient Jewish apocalyptic in general—and for that matter in early Christian apocalyptic in general—the symbols used are, in Wheelwright's terms, steno-symbols; in Ricoeur's, signs rather than symbols. Typically, the apocalyptic seer told the story of the history of his people in symbols where each symbol bore a one-to-one relationship with that which it depicted. This thing was Antiochus IV Epiphanes, that thing was Judas Maccabee, the other thing was the coming of the Romans, and so on. But if this was the case, and it certainly was, then when the seer left the known facts of the past and present to express his expectation of the future his symbols remained steno-symbols, and his expectation concerned singular concrete historical events.

To take an actual example, if in Daniel 11 and 12 the "abomination that makes desolate" is a historical artifact—and it is—and if those who "make many understand" and the "little help" are historically identifiable individuals—and they are—then the "Michael" of Dan 12:1 is also someone who will be historically identifiable, and the general resurrection of Dan 12:2 is an event of the same historical order as the setting up of the altar to Zeus in the Jerusalem temple. The series of events described in Daniel 11 and 12 are events within history; insofar as they are described in symbols, those symbols are steno-symbols (Wheelwright), or they are signs rather than symbols (Ricoeur).

We have now to ask a literary-critical question about the proclamation by Jesus of the Kingdom of God, and it is this. In the proclamation of Jesus, is the apocalyptic symbol "Kingdom of God" in Wheelwright's terms a steno-symbol or a tensive symbol, or to use Ricoeur's distinction, is it a true symbol rather than a sign? Now that question can be answered because on historical-critical grounds it can be established that Jesus *refused to give a sign*. The four Synoptic Gospel passages of Matt 12:39; 16:4; Luke 11:29; Mark 8:11-13 have been examined by my pupil Richard A. Edwards, who has satisfactorily solved the problem of their origins and of the relationship between them, incidentally proving me wrong in the process.[21] He shows that the complex of tradition begins with an account of a refusal by Jesus to give a sign, which account itself is primitive in language and form, and which underlies both Mark and Q. Edwards is himself primarily concerned with the redaction of this primitive pericope in the Q community and by the Synoptic Evangelists. I, however, am concerned with the authenticity of the primitive pericope in which Jesus refuses to give a sign, a pericope now best represented by the Markan version in Mark 8:11-13. I would claim that this pericope is authentic—that is, that it does represent a characteristic of the ministry of the historical Jesus, on the ground (1) that it satisfies the criterion of dissimilarity—Jewish and Christian apocalyptic regularly gives signs; and (2) that it has multiple attestation in the tradition—it underlies both Mark and Q. Moreover, as I argued in my paper at Los Angeles, the particular use of apocalyptic symbolism represented by the refusal to give a sign coheres with what is being expressed in Jesus' distinctive use both of parables and of proverbial sayings.

I, therefore, take it as an established result of historical-critical "Life-of-Jesus Research" that Jesus characteristically refused to give a sign, and in the light of this conclusion I return to the question whether, in the proclamation of Jesus, Kingdom of God is a steno-symbol or a tensive symbol, whether it is a true symbol or only a sign.

This question is no sooner asked than answered because the whole paraphernalia of apocalyptic sign-giving is dependent upon a one-to-one correspondence between the sign/symbol and that which it represents; or, to use Ricoeur's language, its meaning is exhausted in its first, literal intentionality. The essence of apocalyptic sign-giving is to be able to point to one historical person or one historical event and to say that this represents the fulfillment of a previously given apocalyptic symbol. A one-to-one correspondence, a literal intentionality is necessarily implied. But then the steadfast refusal by Jesus to give a sign can be held to imply the opposite—that is, that the symbol "Kingdom of God" is a tensive symbol, that its meaning is by no means exhausted by any "literal intentionality."

This seems to me to be a crucial point about the proclamation of Jesus. In that proclamation "Kingdom of God" is a tensive symbol; it is a true symbol rather than a sign. Last year I offered an exegesis of the crucial "Kingdom sayings" of Jesus—Luke 11:20; 17:20-21; Matt 11:12—based upon the observance of this distinction, and I call attention to that exegesis as strong support for my thesis. I do not propose to repeat that exegesis here, but rather to turn to the consequence of this distinction for the overall interpretation of the proclamation of Jesus, that is, for hermeneutics. If "Kingdom of God" is a steno-symbol or sign in the historical proclamation of Jesus, then our hermeneutical responsibility is earnestly to look for signs of the end and busily to calculate dates for the coming of the Son of Man. But if it is a tensive or true symbol, then our responsibility is to explore the manifold ways in which the experience of God can become an existential reality to people. That the symbol "Kingdom of God" in ancient Israel had reference to the activity of God is fully established. The crux of the distinction now being made is whether in the proclamation of Jesus it has reference to a single identifiable event that every person experiences in his or her own time.

It can be seen that after a somewhat lengthy and circuitous discussion I have ended up essentially where I began, with a Bultmannian understanding of the eschatology of Jesus. But I would regard myself as having advanced beyond Bultmann in one important respect. Bultmann reached the historical-critical decision that Jesus was mistaken in his proclamation of the Kingdom of God. By means of his particular hermeneutical method, however, Bultmann was able to claim that in the "understanding of life" implied by the proclamation of Jesus there was nonetheless something to be taken seriously.

It is my claim today that by approaching Jesus' proclamation of the Kingdom of God from the standpoint of a literary-critical understanding of symbol and the function of symbol, an even more direct interpretation of the message of Jesus into our own time is possible.

There is one further thing to be said, however, and that is in connection with the *function* of symbol. We may have established that "Kingdom of God" is a tensive or true symbol in the message of Jesus, but our hermeneutical task is incomplete if we do not go on to ask: What does such a symbol *do*? What kind of a response does the use of such a symbol *evoke*? I am asking that question not so much in the sense of historical criticism—what *did* it do or evoke in terms of the first century—as in the sense of hermeneutics—what *does* it do or evoke in the terms of the twentieth century? But I ask that question only to have to admit that I have as yet no firm answer to it. I could, of course, echo Paul Ricoeur and say that the symbol gives rise to thought, that the function of a true or tensive symbol is to tease the mind into ever-new evocations of meanings.

This is a valid and important insight. But even as I utter it, I am aware that I am not so much enunciating a principle as announcing a program. One of the tasks to which I believe we have to commit ourselves as biblical scholars is the investigation of the function or evocative power of biblical symbols. This will, of course, take us into the field of psychology and the psychological processes of human understanding; but then one of the characteristics of the contemporary situation in biblical scholarship is that it challenges us to do things that we have not done before. Our situation as biblical scholars is, quite simply, that our traditional understanding of the nature of our task is no longer adequate to its fulfillment. We are all of us trained in historical criticism, and more and more of us are being trained in literary criticism; but if we are to achieve our goal as hermeneuts there is the whole field of human understanding for us to explore.

I must now conclude by summarizing the reflections on method in the interpretation of the New Testament that I have attempted to draw from a discussion of eschatology, specifically the eschatology of Jesus, and hermeneutics. I began by following Bultmann in accepting a definition of hermeneutics as "the art of understanding expressions of life fixed in writing." The first step toward such an understanding of any "expressions of life," I argued, was the task of establishing a historical-critical understanding of it, of establishing, so far as is possible, what the text was intended to say by its author and understood as saying by those to whom it was directed. But this process of arriving at a historical understanding of the text is only the first step in the hermeneutical process.

3

Parables and Hermeneutics

The modern hermeneutical discussion has made us all aware of the ways in which an exegete's presuppositions affect his or her exegesis, and there is no plainer example of this than the exegesis of the parables of Jesus. Here the exegete's theological position, his or her fundamental concern, and methodological presuppositions, can play a surprisingly large role in the way in which the parables are finally understood. The purpose of this article is to illustrate this point in connection with the work of a number of very important interpreters of the parables and then to offer some reflections on the hermeneutical problems thus revealed.

SIX INTERPRETERS OF JESUS' PARABLES

Adolf Jülicher

Let us begin with the father of the modern interpretation of the parables of Jesus, Adolf Jülicher, whose two-volume *Die Gleichnisreden Jesu* (The Parables of Jesus) is still required reading for anyone who intends a serious study of the parables, although perhaps not all 963 pages![1] To read the second volume, or any two hundred pages of it, is to be forced to a series of recognitions. In the first place, one comes to reject allegory once and for all. As Jülicher shows over and over how the allegorizing tendency in the New Testament church and later has obscured an originally vivid and simple picture or story, one finds oneself thinking in terms of cobwebs being swept away. Secondly, the reader becomes convinced of Jülicher's further contention that a parable must have had an original point, and only one, that its first hearers must have been able readily to grasp. Such vivid simplicity cannot have been meant to be obscure in meaning. So far so good.

But then one comes to the meanings that Jülicher himself finds in the various parables. At first they too are convincing; but after a while one begins to wonder. The House Built on Sand (Matt 7:24-27 par.) has the point that hearing and not doing in the case of Jesus' message is as senseless as building a house without bothering about the foundations.[2] The Friend at Midnight (Luke 11:5-8) is intended to encourage the hearers to constancy in prayer,[3] as is The Widow and the Unjust Judge (Luke 18:1-8).[4] The Great Supper (Matt 22:1-14 par.) makes the point that as the feast-giver, so with God; if Jesus' first hearers do not respond, then others will be given the opportunity.[5] The Laborers in the Vineyard (Matt 20:1-16) is concerned with the fact that God has one salvation for all humanity, "for high priest and aristocrat, for tax collector and prostitute."[6] The Sower (Mark 4:3-9, 14-20 par.) is a story to which the hearers would have responded with the recognition that such is indeed the way it is in sowing and harvesting; as they would also have readily made the proper application that it is also the way with the word of God in people's hearts.[7] The Good Samaritan (Luke 10:29-37) teaches that a self-sacrificial act of love is the most valuable thing in human eyes and of God. No privilege of office or birth can take its place.[8]

Each of us should read Jülicher for oneself and make a list; but the result would, I believe, always be the same: about halfway through we become uneasy. In my case at about the conjunction of The Laborers in the Vineyard and The Sower I began to realize that one could put together Jülicher's interpretations of the various parables and come up with a manifesto of nineteenth-century German theological liberalism. At that point I recalled that in the first volume there are some very romantic passages about Jesus' mastery of the parabolic idiom. For example:

> In his parables Jesus has bequeathed to us a masterpiece of popular speech. He is in this area the master; so far as we know no one else has ever approached his achievement. . . . The master is here no one's pupil, he has stolen no one's pen or brush. What he offers is his own creation.[9]

Moreover, among Jülicher's other publications is a classic statement of the relationship between Jesus and the beginnings of Christianity, as this was seen at the height of the German liberal "Life-of-Jesus Research" (*Leben-Jesu-Forschung*).[10] All in all one begins to ask questions about the relationship between Jülicher's theological position as a representative of nineteenth-century German liberalism and his interpretation of Jesus' parables.

Joachim Jeremias

After Jülicher, the next step forward in the interpretation of Jesus' parables to be considered here came through the work of Joachim Jeremias, whose *Para-*

bles of Jesus has developed through the years into the single most important book on the parables and perhaps the greatest single contribution to modern knowledge of the historical Jesus.[11]

Jeremias is self-confessedly concerned to recover the historical words of Jesus because they are, for him, the source of revelation and authority. He is aware of the fact that Albert Schweitzer was able to raise very serious questions about the "quest of the historical Jesus" and that form criticism has made that quest immeasurably more difficult.[12] Nonetheless, he continues it because he is convinced that with proper attention to such things as the historical facts about the thought and life in first-century Palestine (upon which he has spent a lifetime of study and about which he probably knew more than anyone else) and the eschatology of Jesus, Schweitzer's questions can be met. At the same time he welcomes form criticism with its emphasis upon the history of the tradition because it enabled him to write a history of the transmission of the parables in the tradition of the church. His work, in effect, consists of writing a history of the parabolic tradition, establishing the earliest form and then demonstrating the authenticity of many of the parables by means of the criterion of dissimilarity (parable and not allegory, the eschatology of Jesus and not of the early church, etc.), and by means of linguistic and environmental factors (Aramaic language, the situation and conditions of first-century Palestine). Then he interprets the reconstructed original parable by setting it in the context of the ministry of Jesus, and especially in the context of the eschatology of Jesus.[13]

As a sample of his work, let us take his interpretation of The Great Supper (Matt 22:1-14 par.). Jülicher's interpretation of it has been given above. From the versions in Matthew and Luke, Jeremias reconstructed an original story, which the subsequent discovery of the *Gospel of Thomas* proved correct, a story of a feast-giver who filled his banquet hall with beggars after his original guests unanimously rejected an invitation they had initially accepted. This, he then showed, had its roots in a well-known Palestinian story of a rich tax collector and a poor scholar, a story also used in Luke 16:19-31 (The Rich Man and Lazarus). The apparent unreality of the parable—the unanimous rejection of the original invitation by the intended guests and the deliberate invitation of the beggars and homeless in their place—thus becomes explicable in terms of the mores of first-century Palestine on the basis of a well-attested story concerning a rich tax collector, one Bar Ma'yan. Further, there is a note of joy throughout the parable; and its message is:

> God fulfills his promises and comes forward out of his hiddenness. But if the "children of the kingdom," the theologians and the pious circles, pay no heed to his call, the despised and the ungodly will take their place; the others will receive nothing but a "too late" from behind the closed doors of the banquet hall.[14]

What is absolutely typical of Jeremias here is the careful reconstruction of the original, the interpretation in terms of what the first-century Palestinian hearers would have known and taken for granted, and an interpretation in terms of the content of the message of Jesus. So far as the first and second of these things are concerned, he cannot be faulted. The most that the critic could claim is that there are some instances where Jeremias has ascribed to Jesus something that perhaps had its origin in the early church. But such instances would be comparatively few and isolated. It is the third point that concerns us, the interpretation in terms of the content of the message of Jesus. In many ways the most striking thing about Jeremias's book is that he organizes his interpretation of the parables under the heading, "The Message of the Parables of Jesus," and that his interpretation of The Great Supper, for example, comes under the minor rubric, "It May Be Too Late." This is readily understandable in terms of Jeremias's fundamental concern, and it remains a fact that modern reconstructions of the message of Jesus are built upon the parables; but the question has to be raised as to whether there is not rather more to a parable than a contribution to the message of Jesus that can be summarized in a propositional sentence. We shall return to this point below.

Ernst Fuchs

The next scholar we will consider is Ernst Fuchs, who is not so much an exegete as a poet and mystic of the Word, and whose "New Hermeneutic" is both a major contribution to the current hermeneutical scene and a revelation of some aspects of the hermeneutical problem. We will concentrate attention upon his essay, "What Is Interpreted in the Exegesis of the New Testament?"[15] In the first part of this essay Fuchs makes it clear that he is concerned with three separate but related things: a text as produced by a given individual and so representative of that individual's self-understanding; the text itself as intending to say something, to have a meaning; and the reader or hearer as being open or not open to that meaning, as either having or having lost "freedom for the word." All this is a working out of the "language-character" of human existence. These are insights of fundamental importance to the hermeneutical discussion among New Testament scholars, and we shall return to them in the last part of this article.

Against this background Fuchs turns to two parables: The Mustard Seed (Matt 13:31-32 par.) and The Treasure in the Field (Matt 13:44). Unfortunately his characteristic style of expression and discussion now become a hermeneutical barrier, and the relationship between the theoretical principles and their working out in practice becomes difficult to recognize. He does not stay close to the principles he has previously discussed; rather he turns immediately to the assertions that "Jesus . . . did not first explain the *Basileia*

[Kingdom]; he proclaimed its coming." And "Jesus' preaching . . . leads into the future, so that people who previously had no future now have one." Then he claims that the similitude of the mustard seed must not be seen from the beginning forward but from the miracle of the coming of the *Basileia* as the end. "But if the miracle is at the end . . . then the beginning indicates not the miracle but our *relation to* the miracle." So "The *tertium comparationis*" is not "the equation, 'small origin—vast results,' but rather the inverse scheme, 'small stake—vast yield.'" Now the "similitude is no longer a pious address; . . . It has become a text, a preaching text. It gives to these people [the hearers] a context for which they could *not* hope, *nor* even reckon with."[16]

Going on from this interpretation of The Mustard Seed, Fuchs turns to The Treasure in the Field (Matt 13:44) where "the *tertium comparationis* may . . . be formulated as 'large stake—greater yield.'" But the stake is not the hearers', it is Jesus'. "Jesus the preacher is the only one who really invests anything. . . . Jesus . . . risks what he stakes; the audience certainly gains, when they listen to him." Jesus risks his life, or at least this preaching, on his hearers. From this point Fuchs takes off into a consideration of Jesus' word as revelatory event, of *faith* as that which corresponds to this word, and Jesus' love as recognizable in "his pledge for the word addressed in this way."[17]

Reading a Fuchsian exegesis of a parable is to be caught up into a strange new world. Much of what he says is clearly of great importance for the hermeneutical discussion, as, for example, the three separate but related concerns of his preliminary discussion reported above. But much else can be described as only a rhetorical flight of fancy—interesting, even exciting, and often oddly challenging, but nonetheless a flight of fancy. Not since the pre-Jülicher days of allegorizing can an exegete have so used the parables of Jesus as a vehicle for his own ideas. In Fuchs's case those ideas are interesting and even important, but their relationship to the parables of Jesus sometimes seems to be that of an overcoat to the peg it hangs on!

Having said this, however, one has to pause to consider the fact that Fuchs's insights are important enough for him to be taken seriously rather than literally, and that he has had a great influence both upon subsequent interpreters of the parables and upon the hermeneutical discussion among New Testament scholars. In the last part of this article we shall have to concern ourselves intensively with his insights.

Amos N. Wilder

We turn now from Germany to America, to Amos Wilder's *The Language of the Gospel: Early Christian Rhetoric*.[18] This was an epoch-making book for it opened the eyes of the world of New Testament scholarship in America to the significance of general literary criticism for New Testament studies, and today the interaction of literary criticism and biblical criticism is playing an increasingly important role in New Testament studies in America. Wilder was able to make the impact that he did with this book because he is not only a leading biblical scholar in his own right but also a creative literary artist and an experienced literary critic.

So far as the parables are concerned, Wilder devoted one chapter (17 pages!) to them, but the interpretation of the parables was never to be the same again. The first thing to be said about this discussion of the parables is that with masterful ease Wilder achieves one goal toward which Fuchs aimed but which he, in practice, grossly overshot.

> We must go all the way in this matter of context and see them [the parables] in Jesus' own situation. Then their real authority and power emerge. [Concerning The Sower] It is Jesus' own certain faith that paints in the feature of the great harvest. The formal felicity and coherence of these parables reflect the intensity of his own vision.[19]

The extravagant rhetoric of Fuchs's New Hermeneutic has here become the almost instinctive understanding of the creative artist. But perhaps even more important than this for the biblical scholar is the revelation of the significance of the insights of literary criticism.

> Jesus . . . uses tropes or extended images . . . to [mediate] reality and life . . . [to mediate] his own vision and his own faith. This understanding of Jesus' figures of speech is supported by our modern discussion of the metaphor in literary criticism. . . . In the metaphor we have an image with a certain shock to the imagination which directly conveys vision of what is signified.[20]

Further, the parables are strongly realistic; for all their concern with the depths of moral existence and religious life they are earthily secular: "These deeper dimensions are married to such ordinariness and secularity."[21]

The parables Wilder briefly discusses are from Mark 4—The Sower, The Seed Growing of Itself, and The Mustard Seed; and from Matthew 13—The Leaven, The Hidden Treasure, and The Pearl. In this discussion it becomes evident that Wilder's interest is in the creative literary art of the parables and in the effectiveness of that artistry. "Here lies the power and fatefulness of art. [In the parables,] Jesus' speech had the character not of instruction and ideas but of compelling imagination, of spell, of mythical shock and transformation."[22] As usually understood, a parable such as The Sower or The Seed Growing of Itself is banal, an example of what happens every day offered as encouragement. But if we put it in the context of Jesus' situation then everything changes, and it is seen that

> The parable of the sower is a prophetic and not a discursive parable, a metaphor of faith. . . . The disciples are heartened not by a homiletic illustration drawn from nature but by Jesus' impartation to them of his own vision by the power of metaphor.[23]

At this point one begins to recognize the affinity between Wilder's position and concerns and those of the New Hermeneutic of Ernst Fuchs. Indeed, Wilder frequently quotes Fuchs, and to see Fuchs through the clarity of Wilder's vision is to begin to understand him better. What in Fuchs is extravagantly psychological, as well as markedly idiosyncratic in expression, is controlled in Wilder by his instinctive understanding of creative literary art and by the careful application of the discipline of literary criticism. Furthermore, Wilder is as incapable of penning an obscure sentence as Fuchs is of penning a clear one! But there is a sense in which they stand together. Both are concerned in the first place with the fact that one cannot separate an artist from his artistic creation. The parables of Jesus are significant artistic creations and as such they necessarily involve something of the vision, the person, the self-understanding of Jesus himself. Secondly, as artistic creations (what Dan O. Via Jr. was later to call "aesthetic objects") they have a vitality and power of their own. They are able to mediate a new reality—not only to their immediate hearers but to subsequent generations of hearers by means of what Wilder would call the power of metaphor and Fuchs, a "language event." Then, thirdly, the hearers—original or subsequent—are significantly affected by them. In the language of Fuchs, they are either open or not open to the Word; in that of Wilder they not only learn about the reality borne by the metaphor, they participate in it—or refuse to do so.

It can be seen at once that Fuchs and Wilder introduced a new dimension into the discussion of the parables: the dimension of the parable as having an on-going life and vitality of its own. Before going on to subsequent developments in America, however, I must call attention to the concern that Fuchs and Wilder have for the historical Jesus as the author of the parables. The nature of Fuchs's language is such that one tends to dismiss it as excessive psychologizing about Jesus or the like, but in the case of Wilder this cannot be done; for he makes a convincing case for the relationship between the author's vision of reality and the parables themselves. In theological language this might be called "neoliberalism," for it insists on a significant concern for the historical Jesus by the exegete of the parables.[24] Indeed Wilder leaves us in no doubt as to his hermeneutic. Not only are the parables, by the power of metaphor, Jesus' impartation to his disciples of his own vision but "For us, too, to find the meaning of the parable we must identify ourselves with that inner secret of Jesus' faith and faithfulness."[25]

Robert Funk

Once Wilder had called attention to the literary-critical understanding of metaphor and its significance for the exegesis of the parables of Jesus, it was perhaps inevitable that someone would pick up that particular ball and run with it. The scholar who did in fact do so was Robert W. Funk, whose *Language, Hermeneutic, and Word of God* represents a major development in the interpretation of the parables.[26] Funk is concerned with the function of language as such and he has read his Heidegger, Fuchs, and Ebeling—as he has also read Owen Barfield and Philip Wheelwright. The result is the first full-scale discussion of "the parable as metaphor" (the title of chapter 5 of his book) from someone with competence in both biblical and general literary criticism and with a concern for the way in which metaphor functions as metaphor. Although one could wish that he wrote a leaner prose, the fact is that Funk's discussion of the parable as metaphor must now be regarded as required reading for any would-be exegete of the parables—unless, of course, that exegete comes from the world of general literary criticism, in which case Jülicher and Jeremias become the required reading! Funk focuses attention upon the parable as having a life and vitality of its own, simply by reason of the fact that it is metaphor. Now the parable stands in its own right as metaphor, open-ended, capable of transference into a hundred other situations than that of Jesus and his hearers. In their realism the parables show us a world we recognize as our own, but then they suddenly turn that world upside down.

> In saying that parabolic metaphor induces an imaginative grasp of the "world" of the parable by the way in which the everyday world is presented, we are brought, finally, to the explicit consideration of what has been described as vividness or strangeness . . . [Or, again,] the parables as pieces of everydayness have an unexpected "turn" in them which looks through the commonplace to a new view of reality.[27]

It is this element of strangeness in the parables that fascinates Funk. It leads him to interpret The Great Supper as "This never-never-land banquet [which] has quite turned things upside down." And to claim that "Only in fairy tales do beggars sit at the tables of aristocrats, to say nothing of king's tables." Gone is Jeremias's Bar Ma'yan, the Palestinian tax collector who curried God's favor by almsgiving after his failure to curry favor with the notables of his town. In its place is a story from the land of make-believe . . . [which] vibrates in the minds of those who hear . . . [as judgment upon one group and the word of grace to another] judgment and grace are not spoken of directly. . . . Rather, . . . each hearer is drawn into the tale as he wills. . . . The parable identifies each member of the audience, tells each one who he is, and with that the group is split in two.[28]

One has the feeling that Funk is both *right* and *wrong*. He is surely right to resist the reduction of the parables to ideas and to demand that the parable be allowed to be understood as metaphor, open-ended, drawing its hearers into its world and then challenging them in theirs. But if Jeremias's Bar Ma'yan ever existed—and being wrong about such things is not normal for Jeremias!—then the feast in the parable is simply not a "never-never-land banquet."

In the second of the two parables he discusses in detail, The Good Samaritan, Funk is on much firmer ground, for here the element of shock, of topsy-turviness, is surely there in the introduction of the Samaritan. "The Samaritan is brought into a constellation in which he cannot be anticipated. It is this surprising, odd turn which shatters the realism, the everydayness of the story."[29] Moreover, Funk does full justice to the fact that as narrative the parable catches the hearer up into the story, causing him to identify himself with the characters and their situations. Indeed he has a key passage that must be as important as anything ever written about the narrative parables.

Since the metaphor gives itself existentially to unfinished reality, so that the narrative is not complete until the hearer is drawn into it as participant, the hearer is confronted with a situation in relation to which he must decide how to comport himself: is he willing to allow himself to be the victim, to smile at the affront to the priest and Levite, to be served by an enemy? The parable invites, nay, compels him to make some response. And it is this response that is decisive for him. Furthermore, since the parable is temporally open-ended, it is cast onto a plurality of situations, a diversity of audiences, with the consequence that it refuses ideational crystallization. Every hearer has to hear it in *his* own way. The future which the parable discloses is the future of every hearer who grasps and is grasped by his position in the ditch.[30]

A passage such as this is the dawn of a new day in the interpretation of the narrative parables. Now their power as metaphor and their force as narrative is being taken seriously, as is also the fact that they have a life and vitality of their own apart from the original context in the message and ministry of the historical Jesus. Not that Funk is unconcerned with that original context. On the contrary, he wishes to do justice to it and concerns himself concretely with the christological element in the parable. "To put it succinctly, the parable is permission on the part of Jesus to follow him, to launch out into a future that he announces as God's own. In this sense, too, it is christological."[31] But the main burden of his interpretation is clearly elsewhere, and rightly so.

Dan O. Via Jr.

The last interpreter of the parables whose work we will consider is Dan O. Via Jr.[32] Via's work represents a breakthrough because he quite deliberately treats the parables as "aesthetic objects" existing now in their own right and not dependent for their power upon an original historical context. He is concerned with the narrative parables and in fact discusses eight of them: five "tragic" (The Talents, Ten Maidens, Wedding Garment, Wicked Tenants, Unforgiving Servant), and three "comic" (The Workers in the Vineyard, Unjust Steward, Prodigal Son). Where Funk had concerned himself with metaphor, Via concerns himself with the movement of the plot and the roles of the protagonists. In the tragic parables we have "the class of low mimetic, realistic tragedy [in which] we see realistic imagery and ordinary people in dramatic encounters and conflicts moving downward toward catastrophe." In the comic parables, on the other hand, we have "the class of low mimetic, realistic comedy [in which] we view realistic imagery and ordinary people in dramatic, face-to-face confrontations moving upward toward well-being."[33] His concern is to reach the understanding of existence in a parable and then look at the world through that window.

> When we look at the world through the window of the understanding of existence in The Talents, we will have to say that the man who so understands himself that he seeks to avoid risky action rather than trusting God for the well-being of his existence, though he may live long chronologically, will have no present. His time will be evacuated of content.[34]

The Ten Maidens shows us that "The present, then, as time and room to live, is a gift; but it is also a demand. . . . [G]ift and demand are held paradoxically together." The Workers in the Vineyard "suggests to us . . . that the divine dimension may cross our everyday reality to produce a crisis of ultimate importance in the midst of the ordinary.[35] There are similar lessons drawn from each of the eight parables Via discusses.

Via's discussions of the parables themselves are sometimes of quite extraordinary interest, and I am as impressed today by, for example, his treatment of The Unjust Steward as "a miniature of what has come to be known as the picaresque mode" as I was when I first read it.[36] To approach the parables in the way one might approach *Waiting for Godot* seems, in retrospect, an obvious step to take, but the honor indubitably belongs to Via for taking it. At the same time there is a real difference between the obvious force of Via's "literary-existential analysis" and the sometimes quite surprising banality of his "existential-theological interpretation." I noted this in my original review and was puzzled by it; but it was not until I began the preparatory work for this article that I became aware of what I believe to be the reason for it: Via's own methodological presupposition. He explicitly divorces the parable from its historical context, treats it as an "aesthetic object," and approaches it with the methodology of literary criticism. Having done this, he then develops his interpretation. But can the parable finally be treated as an object, as something one stands over against and for which one calmly and dispassionately develops an interpretation? Is there not a sense in which we are caught up into the narrative; a sense in which we find ourselves in the ditch beside the road to Jericho, to plagiarize Funk; a sense in which the parable is suddenly found to be interpreting us, as Fuchs would put it? With these questions we have reached the core of the hermeneutical problem, to some discussion of which we now turn.

The Hermeneutical Problem: Author, Text, and Reader

The interpretation of the parables in modern times offers us a good sampling of the problems and issues raised by the hermeneutical discussion in the area of New Testament studies. Let me indicate what I believe to be revealed by this all too brief review of the work of Jülicher, Jeremias, Fuchs, Wilder, Funk, and Via. In the first place, it becomes clear in considering Jülicher that even though his methodology is sound and scientific, his Jesus speaks with a suspiciously nineteenth-century German accent. Of course in "Life-of-Jesus research" this kind of thing is now so obvious and well-recognized that it is almost a case of "So, what else is new?"

But the lessons *already* learned and *to be* learned from the liberal Life-of-Jesus research are a necessary starting point for any discussion of hermeneutics among New Testament scholars. Jeremias had learned these lessons well and has always been careful to build all kinds of safeguards into his historical exegesis. By and large I would claim that these safeguards have been effective and that Jeremias and those whom he has taught or influenced (I have phrased that deliberately to include Eta Linnemann who, although formally a pupil of Fuchs, is heavily indebted to Jeremias) have now achieved a degree of certainty as to what the parables originally meant or were intended to mean.

So far as historical criticism is concerned, we are now on firm ground with regard to them. But that very success raises a new question: the question as to whether historical criticism and hermeneutics are, in effect, one and the same thing.

This is the issue brought into focus by Fuchs. Fuchs is adumbrating a position in which he is claiming that there are at least three facets to the hermeneutical task. Taking the insights of historical criticism for granted, he goes on to consider:

- The necessary involvement of the author in the created text
- The power of the text itself as a text
- The role of the hearer or reader confronted by that text.

The fact is that here is an insight of fundamental significance. We must assume the results of historical criticism and then go on from there to consider further, and against the constant background of the results of historical criticism, the three facets of what we may call the hermeneutical interaction of author, text, and reader. In the case of the parables, Wilder, Funk, and Via have in effect been developing aspects of this basic insight.

Wilder, as we saw, develops all three aspects. As both creative artist and critic, he recognizes that no artistic creation could exist without the vision of reality that led the original artist to create it and give it its actual form. As literary critic he recognizes both the significance and function of the parables as metaphor. And he then further recognizes the kind of impact they have as metaphor upon the hearer. His treatment is brief but seminal. Funk developed the second and the third aspects of the insight. He concerned himself with the parables as metaphor and the way in which metaphor functions, and with the parables as metaphor extended to narrative that draws the hearer into itself as participant. Via concerned himself with the second aspect of the matter, deliberately disassociating himself from the first and taking up the third only insofar as he developed an interpretation for the reader. In developing the second aspect of the insight, he concerned himself with the form and function of the parables as narrative, with plot and protagonists, rather than with the power of narrative to draw in the hearer as participant. The lesson would seem to be that both are necessary.

Historical Criticism

The first thing to become evident out of all this in connection with the hermeneutical problem is the relevance of historical criticism. The limitations of historical criticism are such that it must be regarded as the beginning and not the end of the hermeneutical task, but its strength is such that if any tension arises between its results and other aspects of our hermeneutical method then it tends to assert itself. So, for example, if Jeremias is right about Bar Ma'yan and The Great Supper, then Funk's interpretation of that parable in terms of a never-never-land banquet becomes dubious. For all that, Funk may well be right about the element of surprise in metaphor.

The point to be made is that historical criticism does justice to the particularity of that one parable and as such takes precedence over a general point. At the same time historical criticism does not always exercise that element of control. It may well be true, for example, that many of the parables of Jesus were originally weapons of controversy directed against particular groups of opponents as Jeremias has claimed. But does that mean that they must always be interpreted in that particular historical context? The answer this time is in the negative; but then at this point we have reached a limit of historical criticism by observing that an aesthetic object created in one situation for one purpose can take on a life and vitality of its own as it moves into other situations, and this is certainly true of the parables of Jesus. The problem of the strength and limitations of historical criticism, of its relevance and irrelevance for the hermeneutical task, is one with which we are clearly going to have to wrestle, and not only in connection with the parables.

Authorship

The next point to arise is that of the relevance of the original act of authorship to the subsequent interpretation of a parable, the first facet of Fuchs's threefold insight. This point has been much discussed in general literary criticism; but rather than to enter into that discussion, it will be better for our purpose to stay within our deliberately chosen confines of a discussion of these six modern interpretations of the parables and what we learn from them. Here we come face-to-face with the issue in the work of Amos Wilder with its claim that Jesus imparted his vision to his disciples by the power of metaphor and that we must identify ourselves with that inner secret of Jesus' faith and faithfulness. As I intimated above, I am fully prepared to plagiarize James M. Robinson and call that neoliberalism, but the question is not what we may call it but whether we may regard it as justified.

On the one side there is the undisputed fact that the parables are given their homogeneity, and no little of their power, because they do indeed effectively give expression to the creative vision of reality—of the world, humanity, and God—which inspired them. Since that is the case, we can no more interpret them adequately without reference to that vision than we could interpret the Gettysburg Address without reference to Lincoln's vision of the reality that was to become the United States of America. But then there is another side. For one thing, we have all become so aware of the inadequacies of theological liberalism in the field of hermeneutics that if it is a case of once bitten, twice shy, then we are twenty times shy. Then again, the pyrotechnical psychologizing of an Ernst Fuchs is enough to sound alarm bells all over the place. Finally, and most important of all, we face the almost insuperable difficulties of knowing very much about the inner secret of the faith and faithfulness of a man from another place and another time for whom we have no autobiographical sources. All in all we can only say that this is another problem with which we are going to have to wrestle.

Force and Function

The third point to arise is that of the force and function of a text because of the particular form it has as a text—in the case of the parables, the force and function of metaphor and of metaphor extended to narrative. This is the point adumbrated in the second aspect of Fuchs's threefold insight but given its effective development in the work of Wilder, Funk, and Via. Here the work is so obviously effective that it carries immediate conviction. An understanding of what metaphor is and how it works, of what kind of language metaphorical language is and how it functions; a literary-critical understanding of both the internal dynamics of narrative (Via) and of its ability to catch up the hearer as participant (Funk)—clearly all this has radically affected the interpretation of the parables of Jesus.

We are face-to-face with an aspect of our hermeneutical task here that we are only just beginning to understand; and it would be hard to exaggerate its importance. A homogeneous text has a certain form and that form functions in a certain kind of way; it is written in a certain kind of language and that language has a particular kind of force and not another. This is what we begin to see through the interpretation of the parables by Wilder, Funk, and Via; and once we have seen it there is clearly no going back from it. To give but one minor example: If it is true that the unjust steward is a "picaresque rogue" and the prodigal son a "picaresque saint," as Via claims they are, then the modern understanding of the way such literary creations function is a valid and indeed indispensable aid to the interpretation of The Unjust Steward and The Prodigal Son respectively. So far we have only taken a few preliminary steps in this direction, but I would certainly claim that this is the direction in which our work should move and indeed in which it is moving.

Text and Interpreter

Then lastly, there arises the point of the dynamic interaction between text and interpreter. There is a sense in which not only does the interpreter interpret the text; the text in turn interprets the interpreter. The modern interpretation of the parables of Jesus we have reviewed makes this clear in a number of ways: the way in which presuppositions of various kinds play an important role in interpretation; Fuchs's insight about the hearers' openness for the word, or lack of it; Funk's vivid picture of the hearer in the ditch by the Jericho road. Of course this point is not new in New Testament studies; Bultmann has made us relentlessly aware of it through the years. But again it is a point that has proven obdurate. Other people's presuppositions are always so much easier to recognize than our own; and, more important, the dividing line between dispensable presupposition and indispensable hermeneutical principle is extremely difficult to draw as we saw in the case of Wilder's concern for Jesus' faith and faithfulness.

But this point of dynamic interaction between text and interpreter is the heart of the hermeneutical enterprise and worth our every effort to understand. In a sense, everything else we have discussed comes into play here: the questions of historical intent and purpose, of the vision of the author, of the literary and linguistic form of the text. All this can and must help us to come to the text of a parable with the kind of openness the parable itself demands, or, as Bultmann would put it, with the kind of questions the parable intends to answer.

CONCLUSION

But mention of Bultmann's point reminds us that the hermeneutical discussion among New Testament scholars has now gone beyond Bultmann, in no small part because of the insights achieved and expressed by Ernst Fuchs. In his essay deliberately dedicated to Bultmann we find an emphasis upon the "language-character" of human existence. Without allowing ourselves to be detoured into a consideration of the earlier and later Heidegger, we may say that for Bultmann a text with meaning (to use Fuchs's phrase) offers answers to the fundamental questions of human existence that the interpreter brings to it; whereas for Fuchs that text expresses an aspect of the meaning of human existence that makes its impact upon the interpreter precisely because of the linguisticality of human existence.

What has happened since Bultmann is that we have become aware of what Fuchs calls the language character of human existence, of the ways in which human existence is linguistically determined; and this clearly has very considerable hermeneutical consequences. There are many different artistic forms in which the reality of human existence can be expressed—a Gothic cathedral, for example, a Beethoven symphony, Picasso's *Guernica*, the moods and sounds of African American music—but the linguisticality of human existence is such that an expression in words is the most immediate, and the one broadest and most lasting in impact. Because of this a text with meaning, a linguistic expression of the reality of human existence, necessarily has a special kind of impact upon the reader whose existence is linguistically determined. This is certainly true of the parables of Jesus, and it is a further aspect of the hermeneutical discussion upon which our attention must be focused in the future.

It would be my claim here that the outlines of a viable hermeneutical method to be used in connection with the parables is beginning to emerge. It must give due place to historical criticism and its results, and it must pay proper attention to each of the three facets of the hermeneutical endeavor to which Fuchs called attention and which Wilder, Funk, and Via have so dramatically developed, to what I have called the hermeneutical interaction of author, text, and reader.

4

The Evangelist as Author

This seems to me to be an appropriate occasion to reflect in general terms on the question of *method* in the study and interpretation of the Synoptic Gospels and Acts (SGA). There is perhaps now also a specific need to do this because in recent years we have had something of an explosion in method in connection with the study and interpretation of these texts, and we need to pause for a moment and think through what we are doing. The explosion in method to which I refer is, of course, the rapid development of redaction criticism and the ramifications it is proving to have for our understanding of the Evangelists and the nature and extent of their literary activity. Let me put this matter in perspective by reviewing very briefly some well-known facts about the development of New Testament scholarship in connection with the SGA.

HISTORY OF METHODS

Source Criticism

The first major era of this scholarship may be called the "era of source criticism." It began about the middle of the nineteenth century, in no small part as a response to the challenge of David Friedrich Strauss and his *Das Leben Jesu, kritisch bearbeitet* in 1935–36 (ET: *The Life of Jesus, Critically Examined,* 1973), and lasted until the First World War.[1] For a variety of reasons—the urge to demolish Strauss's mythical view of the Gospel narrative, the stimulus of the developing historical sciences, the fact that most New Testament critics were of a liberal theological persuasion—the era of source criticism was also the era of viewing the Evangelists as essentially chroniclers of the ministry of Jesus and, in the case of Luke-Acts, of the history of the early church.

So the Gospel of Mark was esteemed, not only as prior to those of Matthew and Luke, but also as an essentially historical account of the ministry of Jesus, while the hypothetical second source for Matthew and Luke, the Sayings Source designated "Q," was regarded as an essentially accurate record of the message of Jesus. The one prophetic voice raised against this view of the Evangelists was, of course, that of William Wrede, who in 1901 argued that the Evangelist Mark had a thematic concern for the Messianic Secret and that, far from being a historical chronicle, his work was actually the first chapter of a history of Christian origins.[2]

Form Criticism

The second major era of New Testament scholarship in connection with the SGA began after the First World War with the rise of form criticism in Germany. At this point the chronology gets somewhat confused because form criticism was somewhat strenuously resisted by a whole generation of scholars outside of Germany, with such notable exceptions as R. H. Lightfoot in England and F. C. Grant and B. S. Easton in America.[3] But in retrospect we may speak of the era between the First and Second World Wars as the "era of form criticism."

Form criticism accepted the literary results of the era of source criticism, the Two-Source Hypothesis, but not that era's view of the Evangelists. It concerned itself with the oral tradition that preceded the Gospels and the Sayings Source, and that continued to exist alongside the written documents. It examined the forms to be found in this tradition, their function as forms in the early Christian communities, and their history in the tradition of those communities. It saw the Gospels as consisting very largely of traditional material that had had a shorter or longer history of use in the Christian communities, and that in no small part had been created for that use. And it saw the Evangelists as essentially collectors and editors of this material. The Evangelists were no longer chroniclers of the ministry of Jesus: they were collectors and editors of traditional material that had had a distinct function in the life situation of the Christian communities, and they were by no means always masters of that material.

This last point is important. The two most important of the pioneer form critics, Rudolf Bultmann and Martin Dibelius, had a comparatively low estimate of the Evangelists as authors.[4] And they taught a whole generation of scholars to be prepared to think of the Evangelists primarily as responding to forces at work in the Christian communities rather than as creative literary figures, and of the Gospels as probably containing large and important elements of comparatively undigested traditional material, rather than as homogeneous wholes.

It is interesting to note in this connection that the form critics distinguished quite sharply between the Gospel of Luke and the Acts of the Apostles, between the author "Luke" as he worked on the Gospel of Luke and as he worked on the Acts of the Apostles. We must retrace our steps a little to see the reasons for this. The era of source criticism produced a general consensus with regard to the Synoptic Gospels, the Two-Source Hypothesis. All through that same era, and indeed down to the present, very considerable scholarly effort has been expended to discover similarly extensive sources for the Acts of the Apostles. It was natural enough to assume that if the author "Luke" had used extensive sources in the case of his Gospel, then he would have done the same with regard to his Acts of the Apostles. In the case of the Acts of the Apostles, however, no consensus with regard to sources ever developed; it was found that the existence of a major source, such as Mark or Q in the case of the Gospel, could neither be demonstrated nor even convincingly argued from the text of Acts.

In the era of form criticism this same disparity between the Gospel of Luke and the Acts of the Apostles continued. The pioneer form critic Martin Dibelius turned his attention to Acts but he could find there very little of the kind of traditional material he had found so abundantly in the Gospels, including the Gospel of Luke. Nor could he find any model for Acts in the sense that the Gospel of Mark is a model for the Gospel of Luke. Dibelius's conclusion was that "Luke" had gone to work in quite a different manner in the case of Acts than he had in the case of his Gospel, and the consequence of this conclusion is that the title of Dibelius's fundamental work on Acts does not imitate that of his fundamental work on the Gospels, *Die Formgeschichte der Evangelien* (Form Criticism of the Gospels). We do not have "Die Formgeschichte der Apostelgeschichte" (Form Criticism of the Book of Acts), but rather "Stilkritisches zur Apostelgeschichte" ("Style Criticism of the Book of Acts").[5] The key to understanding Acts is not form criticism but style criticism. In the case of Acts, "Luke" exercises the literary freedom of an author in a way that he does not in the case of his Gospel. As Dibelius himself puts it, "Here, then, the author can fashion the material he has collected as far as it permits; he can select, abbreviate, or elaborate; he determines the sequence of events; he creates collecting links and independent passages in between."[6] In other words, he is an author working with traditional material.

Dibelius's work on Acts bore fruit in the form of Ernst Haenchen's commentary, in which we find a long essay, and a very good one, on "Luke as Theologian, Historian, Writer."[7] We also find, for example, the three accounts of Paul's conversion are accounted for, not in terms of differing sources or traditional forms, but in terms of differing literary purposes of the author in each particular instance.

Redaction Criticism

With the rapid development of redaction criticism the same attitude as that developed by Dibelius and Haenchen with regard to Luke as the author of Acts is being developed with regard to Matthew, Mark, and Luke as the authors of the Synoptic Gospels. We are becoming more and more sensitive to the fact that the Evangelists are authors working freely and creatively with their material. I would like to make the point in this way: We are becoming aware that Luke is every bit as much an author in the case of the Gospel of Luke as he is in the case of Acts. He is nonetheless an author because he has a model for the Gospel, which he does not have for Acts; he is nonetheless free because he has more extensive traditional material in the one case than in the other. As a good New Testament scholar should, let me illustrate this point from the text of Luke-Acts.

In Mark 1:9-11 we have an account of the Baptism of Jesus, and that is what it is: an account of a baptism. In Luke 3:21-22 Luke is following Mark, and we have a pericope that is uniformly titled "The Baptism of Jesus." But that is exactly what it is not. The verb describing the baptism is carefully linked with two other verbs, one describing a general baptism and one calling attention to the fact that Jesus was praying, and all three are equally carefully subordinated to the action of the main verbs, which describe the Descent of the Spirit upon Jesus. The Baptism has become The Descent of the Spirit. We do not know the form or extent of the traditional material that Luke uses at the beginning of Acts. What we do know, however, is that he takes care to establish an exact parallel between the beginning of the ministry of the Spirit through Jesus and the beginning of the ministry of the Spirit through the church. Just as in the Gospel the Baptism of Jesus becomes the Descent of the Spirit upon him, so in Acts the Descent of the Spirit upon the church at Pentecost (Acts 2:1-13) is carefully interpreted as a Baptism (Acts 1:5).

This careful parallelism of the stories told at the beginning of the Gospel of Luke and the Acts of the Apostles respectively is followed by an equally careful parallelism in terms of the total structure of each work. Each of them is carefully divided into two parts by means of a distinctive literary device: a mental resolve on the part of the leading protagonist in the plot. In Luke 9:51 Jesus "sets his face" to go to Jerusalem and his ascension; and in Acts 19:21 Paul resolves that it is necessary for him "to see Rome." Then in each case the author develops his work in accordance with these indications of its structure and of the outcome of its plot. Whether a reference to the ascension should be read in Luke 24:51 or not—and in view of the literary device in Luke 9:51 I think it should be—it is clear that the ascension of Jesus is the dividing line between the ministry of the Spirit through Jesus and the ministry of the Spirit through the apostles. Similarly the account of Paul preaching openly and unhindered in Rome marks the transition from the story of the apostles to the story of the church of Luke's own readers. I would claim that Luke has exercised the freedom of an author both in regard to the Gospel and to Acts. The fact that he has inherited a traditional model and traditional material has not noticeably inhibited his freedom and creativity as an author.

One could of course reinforce this point by making further observations with regard to the Gospel of Luke and Acts, and one could make a similar point with regard to the Gospel of Matthew; but it is not necessary to do so. I may simply claim that the logical consequence of our more recent work is the conclusion that the Evangelists Matthew and Luke have exercised the creative freedom of genuine authors with regard both to their model and their material. If this is true of Matthew and Luke, then it is certainly true of Mark. Whatever may have been the nature of the model Mark is following, whatever may have been the form or extent of the traditional material he is using, he is certainly exercising the creative freedom of an author.

Literary Criticism

The consequence of recent developments in the study of the SGA has been, then, the recognition that the Evangelists are genuinely authors, authors using traditional material but nonetheless authors: they write for a definite purpose, they give their work a distinct and individual structure, they have thematic concerns that they pursue, the characters in the story they each tell function as protagonists in a plot, and so on. But if this is the case, and I am claiming that it is, then this means that we have to introduce a whole new category of criticism into our study of the SGA, the category of general literary criticism. If the Evangelists are authors, then they must be studied as authors, and they must be studied as other authors are studied. In connection with the SGA, "literary criticism" has normally meant the consideration of sources and literary relationships. But we are going to have to widen our concern to cover every aspect of the work of the Evangelists as authors.

Having said this, however, I want to make it quite clear that I do not mean that we should abandon the time-honored and proven methods developed for the study of the SGA. We are not going to abandon source criticism, or the study of the literary relationships between the Gospels. And form criticism and redaction criticism in its narrower sense of the study of the redaction of existing tradition will remain absolutely indispensable to us. What I am urging is that we add to these things the insights and concerns that stem naturally from the realization that the Evangelists are authors. In this connection the absolutely fundamental fact of life is that any literary criticism has to be geared specifically to the nature of the texts with which it is concerned. There is no universally valid critical method by means of which we can effectively study any given text.

I regard this point as one of the greatest possible importance. Literary critics who work on the SGA will have to develop a form of criticism that is geared specifically to the nature of the SGA. They will need to learn from other literary critics whose primary competence lies elsewhere, in other genres of literature. But in the last resort, there is a form of criticism that applies specifically to the SGA.

A Methodology for Literary Criticism and the Gospels

What would it look like, this form of literary criticism developed specifically in connection with the SGA? With this question we come to the heart of this paper, for it is my purpose today to reflect precisely on this point. I am of course using the terms "literary criticism" and "method in study and interpretation" as synonyms. I began by using the term "method in study and interpretation" because I felt I had to lay the groundwork for the use of the term "literary criticism" in a much broader sense than it normally has among New Testament scholars. In my view, literary criticism in connection with the SGA should have the following features.

Text and Language

It goes without saying that we must continue the concerns that have been an integral part of our scholarship from its beginning: textual criticism and the study of the languages of the New Testament.[8] I mention these things first because I want to make it quite clear that I regard them as absolutely essential, as we all do. But I shall not dwell upon them because they are so thoroughly established and their place in our discipline is so sure that I need do no more than mention them.

Source Criticism

Similarly in need of no more than a mention is source criticism. I take it as an assured result of our work in this area that the Two-Source Hypothesis is valid for the Synoptic Gospels and that there are no major connected sources for the Acts of the Apostles.[9] At the same time, I am glad that these questions are reopened from time to time because it challenges me to think through again and perhaps to refine some details of our hypothesis.

Historical Location

This is another concern that we have inherited from the past. Ever since the time of Ferdinand Christian Baur and the "Tübingen School" of a century and more ago, we have recognized the fact that the works that make up the New Testament were produced in concrete historical situations and addressed to concrete historical questions.[10] So the SGA have definite places in the spectrum of the history of New Testament Christianity, and they must be understood and interpreted in their historical contexts.[11]

Although this point has been recognized as valid for more than a century, it needs more than a mention here. In the first place, I want to make it quite clear that we should be conscious of what we are doing. We are saying in effect that for all the timeless validity of these works, they were in fact written under decidedly temporal circumstances, and that any valid interpretation of them must take their concrete historical contexts seriously into account. Now this is an important hermeneutical principle, and it is by no means a self-evident one. For centuries the SGA were in fact interpreted without any regard for their original historical context, and there are literary critics who are fully persuaded that texts can be and perhaps even should be interpreted without reference to their original historical context. This view has recently surfaced among New Testament scholars in connection with the parables of Jesus. This is a matter that requires careful discussion in connection with all the works that make up the New Testament, and I do not intend to foreclose that discussion in advance when I say that we must take the original historical context of the SGA seriously into account. It is clearly our scholarly task to set the SGA as firmly as we can in their original historical context whatever we may decide about the significance of our knowledge of that historical context in the final hermeneutical task.

Before leaving this point let me remind you that an impressive recent development in New Testament scholarship has been the way in which we have been able to determine the original historical contexts of the SGA: the circumstances that called them forth, the questions to which they are addressed, and the purposes of their authors in writing them. I may perhaps be allowed to illustrate this with reference to the Gospel of Mark. This Gospel was written during a period of resurgence of apocalyptic, a resurgence of apocalyptic precipitated by the First Judean Revolt (66–70 C.E.). This was accompanied in the communities for which the author writes by a false understanding of Christology and hence of the nature of Christian discipleship. A major concern of the author is to controvert this false understanding, and this concern he pursues in two main ways: (1) by subordinating everything to the passion and reinterpreting both Christology and Christian discipleship in light of the passion; and (2) by the literary device of putting the false understanding on the lips of the disciples and the true understanding on the lips of Jesus. In this connection the presentation of Peter in the narratives is particularly important. The author's overall understanding of things is a deeply apocalyptic one. He sees himself and his readers as involved in the third act of an apocalyptic drama that is hurrying toward its climax. The first act was the mission of John the Baptist, and this act ended with the "delivering up" (using a technical term *paradidonai*) of the Baptist (Mark 1:14).[12] The second act began with the preaching of the gospel by Jesus (1:14) and ended with Jesus himself being "delivered up" (again using *paradidonai:* 9:31; 10:33). The third act began with the preaching of the gospel of Jesus Christ, the Son of God, by the church (1:1) and ended with the "delivering up" of the believers (again using *paradidonai:* 13:9, 11, 12) and the imminently expected coming of Jesus as Son of Man (13:26). We can now make similar statements abut the historical context and purpose of the Gospel of Matthew and of the two-volume Luke-Acts, and I have in fact done this in my *The New Testament: An Introduction.*[13] Clearly our ability to do this with real force and clarity marks a new stage in the historical interpretation of the SGA.

Form Criticism

A further aspect of the literary criticism of the SGA that we have inherited from the past, in this case the more immediate past, is form criticism.[14] This was the dominant theme in the criticism of the SGA in the period between the two world wars, and it remains an absolutely essential element of our critical method today. We are indebted to form criticism for our understanding of the nature and extent of the traditional material that the authors of the SGA have used, and there can obviously be no valid study and interpretation of their work that is not thoroughly steeped in the insights and methodology of form criticism. Nor may we by any means assume that all the form-critical discoveries have now been made and all the form-critical insights already developed. Such recent events as Ernst Käsemann's work on what he liked to call "Sentences of Holy Law" and I would much prefer to call "Eschatological Judgment Pronouncements,"[15] the flood of light thrown upon the form of the use of the Old Testament in the New Testament, and least in the SGA, by the discovery of Qumran commentaries (*pesharim*), and the very important current discussion of the influence of the aretalogy upon the gospel form as a whole—all of this is an indication of the fact that literary critics of the SGA must be, and must continue to be, form critics.

But having said that I must return to the point I tried to make earlier, namely, that we cannot any longer accept the comparatively low estimate of the Evangelists as authors that was characteristic of the work of Bultmann and Dibelius. Today the Evangelists must be seen as authors who made extensive use of traditional material. While it is the discipline of form criticism that helps us to understand the nature and extent of that material, that discipline must not be allowed to inhibit our appreciation of the creativity of the Evangelists as authors. A similar thing is true in the case of the question of a model for the Gospels as literary wholes. The Evangelists Matthew and Luke certainly had as a model the Gospel of Mark, but that did not notably inhibit their creative freedom in the use of it. We do not know as yet what model or models the Evangelist Mark may have had, but we can say that his Gospel itself is the result of an act of literary creativity and must be studied and interpreted as such.

Redaction Criticism

With redaction criticism we reach the present day, for the major feature of current work on the SGA is the use of this methodological development.[16] Since the Evangelists are authors using traditional materials, it is important to study their particular use of these materials. This is what redaction criticism was concerned to do. Form criticism had taught us that the Evangelists had used traditional material; redaction criticism set out to study their editorial use of this material. As is well known, the discipline was given its name in Germany as *Redaktionsgeschichte* (redaction history), and the German word *Redaktor* means "editor." The discipline got off the ground in works that observed the redaction of Mark and the Sayings Source Q by the Evangelists Matthew and Luke. But it has proven possible to extend the characteristic method to the Evangelist Mark as well. By a sophisticated combination of observation of linguistic features, compositional techniques, and thematic concerns it is possible to separate tradition from redaction, and hence to observe the redactional process even in the case of the Gospel of Mark. In passing, however, I may be permitted to remark that in the case of the Gospel of Mark it is the combination of features that counts. The work of the SBL Task Force on Mark has, I believe, shown rather convincingly that linguistic features alone are not sufficient to separate tradition from redaction.

The observation of the Evangelists' redaction of traditional material has proven to be most a fruitful method for arriving at their characteristic concerns and emphases, and redaction critics are rewriting the book so far as the theology of the SGA are concerned. But once we began to determine the characteristic theology and concerns of the Evangelists by observing their literary activity in editing and arranging traditional material, there was obviously no point in restricting ourselves in our consideration of this literary activity to the observation of their redaction of the tradition. Any form of the Evangelists' literary activity that we could observe would be equally important, and the next step, therefore, was clearly indicated: we had to concern ourselves with the literary activity of the Evangelists above and beyond their redaction of tradition. This is of course what did happen, especially perhaps here in America.

At this point I would like to pause for a moment to point out that what happened in effect was that redaction criticism taught us to see the Synoptic Evangelists as authors. First they were seen primarily as chroniclers of the ministry of Jesus to be esteemed according to how well they had recorded the facts. Then they were seen primarily as collectors of tradition, by no means necessarily masters of their material. But with the coming of redaction criticism all this changed and we could see them for what they were: authors using extensive amounts of traditional material. Once we had seen them in that light, then there was absolutely no reason for us to limit our conception of their authorial activity to the redaction of tradition. Nor did we in fact do so. We moved on to the things that will concern me for the remainder of this essay. None of the things we shall discuss were actually new, but they did achieve a new prominence and importance as a result of the rise of redaction criticism.

Composition and Structure

There has of course always been some concern for the composition and structure of the SGA. So far as the Gospel of Mark is concerned, for example, Ernst Lohmeyer in Germany and R. H. Lightfoot in England had been interested in this aspect of the matter,[17] with the result that redaction criticism inherited a number of important insights: Mark's use of the compositional technique of intercalation, the use of the two giving of sight stories to set off the central section of the Gospel (Mark 8:27—10:45), the function of that section in the structure of the Gospel as a whole, and so on. Then, in the case of the Gospel of Matthew, Benjamin W. Bacon had pointed to the five great discourses with their formula-like endings and argued a point about the Matthew theology from their function in the Gospel as a whole.[18] Then in the case of Acts, it had been observed that the overall structure of the work corresponds to the program outlined in the missionary commission of Acts 1:8. Despite all this, however, it is fair to say that until redaction criticism opened our eyes to the Evangelists as authors, this aspect of the study and interpretation of their work was not adequately pursued. It is perhaps indicative of the pre-redaction critical state of mind that Ernst Haenchen's commentary on Acts, itself a pioneering work in its treatment of Luke as an author, pays little attention to the structure of the work and simply comments on it pericope by pericope, in sequence![19]

This comparative neglect of composition and structure is the more surprising in light of the obvious fact that an ancient author simply did not have the modern method of giving a structure to his work by means of a table of contents, chapter divisions, headings, etc. The indications of the intended structure had therefore to be internal, presented within the text itself. But the point is that prior to the rise of redaction criticism we were not thinking seriously enough of the Evangelists as authors and hence not looking seriously enough for internal indices of their authorial intent in the works they wrote. All this has now changed and today we concern ourselves as never before with such literary devices as summary reports, geographical references, formula quotations, intercalation and tautologous repetition, as well as with statements of purpose on the part of the chief protagonists and explicit commands on the part of the risen Lord. All of these and other literary devices have been used by the Evangelists to give form and structure to their work, and we must pay careful attention to them if we are to see the SGA as their authors intended them to be seen.

A consequence of this new concern for the composition and structure of the SGA is the growing recognition of the necessity to interpret any part of one of these works in terms of its function within the structure of the work as a whole. This has come into focus, for example, in connection with the Gospel of Matthew where both Jack Kingsbury's *The Parables of Jesus in Matthew 13* and William Thompson's *Matthew's Advice to a Divided Community* give evidence of its fruitfulness.[20] The fact to be recognized is that the SGA are carefully structured works within which the authors have given indications of their intended structures by means of various literary devices. It follows, therefore, that no interpretation of any pericope within, or section of, these works can be adequate that does not raise questions about the place and function of that pericope or section within the structure of the work as a whole.

Protagonists and Plot

It had long been recognized the "the Jews" in the Gospel of John did not correspond to any ethnic group at the time of Jesus, and that "the disciples" in the Gospel of Mark were not simply the group that gathered around Jesus during his ministry in Galilee and Judea. But with the growing realization of the fact that the Evangelists are authors we are free to explore in a new way the function of groups and individuals as protagonists in the plot of each individual work.

Let me make it quite clear that I am claiming that each of the Gospels has a distinct plot. True, both Matthew and Luke follow the broad outline of the Gospel of Mark, but they introduce such considerable variations of their own that each story has its own distinctive features. It is not too much to say that within the broad outline of a movement from a baptism by John in the Jordan River to a death on a cross outside Jerusalem, each Evangelist presents a distinctive version of the story with a plot of its own. Moreover the characters function quite differently in each version of the story. Neither the disciples nor Peter play the same role in the Gospel of Matthew that they play in the Gospel of Mark. And the Jesus of Luke's Gospel is a paradigm of Christian piety in a way that he is not in the other Synoptic Gospels.

The case for the fact that the individuals and groups in the SGA function as protagonists in a plot has been strengthened by Theodore J. Weeden's appeal to Marrou's study of education in antiquity, and his subsequent treatment of the disciples as they function as characters in the Markan drama.[21] Weeden has shown, in effect, that once we begin to think of the Evangelists as authors we must go on to think in terms of characters and dramatic plot, for this is the way in which readers were trained to think in antiquity. So we may—and indeed we must—recognize that the authors of the SGA are using the disciples and Peter, the various groups among the Jews, the figures of Peter and Paul in the early church, and so on, as protagonists and antagonists in the plot of the story they intend to tell. A general literary critic might be surprised that I should find it necessary to emphasize a point that he or she would consider self-evident; but New Testament scholars have generally inherited a rather different understanding of the nature of the narratives of the SGA.

Themes

The fact that the Synoptic Evangelists pursued themes was of course first recognized by William Wrede, who in 1901 isolated the theme of the messianic secret in the Gospels. But like the other things we are talking about the recognition of the thematic concerns of the authors of the SGA is something that has come much more into prominence since redaction criticism freed us to consider the Synoptic Evangelists as authors. Today it is natural for us to consider the Evangelist Mark not only as pursuing the theme of the messianic secret, but also as having a thematic concern for a particular understanding of Christology and of Christian discipleship, as having a concern for a particular understanding of eschatology, and as indulging in an anti-Jerusalem polemic in the last part of his Gospel. The Evangelist Matthew and the author of Luke-Acts are also recognized today as having thematic concerns. I will give only an obvious example in each case. The Evangelist Matthew pursues the theme of religion as essentially obedience to an authoritatively interpreted verbal revelation. To this end he arranges the major aspects of the message of Jesus into five discourses, in imitation of the five books of the Torah, and he carefully restricts the activity of *teaching* to Jesus until the post–Resurrection scene of the Great Commission, in which the disciples are specifically commissioned to *teach*, i.e., authoritatively to interpret the verbal revelation. The author of Luke-Acts pursues the theme "From Jerusalem to Rome." Jerusalem is the place of the passion of Jesus and a major feature of the narrative of the Gospel of Luke is the journey of Jesus to Jerusalem (Luke 9:51, for example). In Acts, Jerusalem is the place of the passion of Stephen and of the persecution of the church, and the whole narrative of Acts is concerned with the theme, "From Jerusalem to Rome." In Acts 1:8 the risen Lord commissions the disciples for a mission from Jerusalem to Rome and the narrative of Acts carefully follows this scheme. In Acts 19:21 Paul's resolve to "see" Rome functions precisely as does Jesus' "setting his face" to go to Jerusalem in Luke 9:51—it determines the course of the remainder of the narrative. Most spectacularly of all, each of the three accounts of Paul's conversion in Acts—now, thanks to Haenchen, to be recognized as deliberate literary creations of the author—features a commission to go into the wider world of Rome, while at the same time insisting, against all historical probability, that Paul's witness virtually began in Jerusalem. It is clear that the authors of the SGA consciously pursue thematic concerns.

It has been the purpose of this essay to argue that "Matthew," "Mark," and "Luke" are authors who make extensive use of traditional material and that this fact has implications for the appropriate critical method to be used in the study and interpretation of their work. I have sought to develop in broad outline what seems to me to be the appropriate critical method, the form of literary criticism geared to the specific nature of the texts. It will be obvious of course that I have limited myself quite deliberately to the critical method involved in interpreting the text historically, and I am very well aware that this is only the beginning and not the end of the hermeneutical task. But there can be, in my view, no valid hermeneutics that does not consider seriously the intent of the author and the original purpose of the text that he created.

5

The Interpretation of the Gospel of Mark

The interpretation of the Gospel of Mark today requires a sophisticated, eclectic method of approach, a method I would call *literary criticism* to distinguish it from the narrower *redaction criticism*. In an attempt to show why this is the case, I will review the various methodological approaches to the Gospel that have been practiced since the rise of the modern scholarly concern for it. I will then develop some of the features of a literary criticism that might be applied to the Gospel.

FROM WREDE TO LOHMEYER

The Historicizing Approach

It is well known that the Gospel of Mark was neglected for centuries because it was regarded as little more than an abbreviation of Matthew. When it became a major object of scholarly concern in the late nineteenth century it did so for two reasons—one valid and one invalid. It came to be regarded as the earliest of the Gospels, which it was, and as fundamentally a historical chronicle of the ministry of Jesus, which it was not. But the historicizing approach appeared to make sense of certain surface characteristics of the Gospel, the outline of the story, the realism of the narratives, the naturalism of the presentation of Jesus, and so on. Moreover, it was supported by the ancient ecclesiastical tradition linking the Evangelist with the apostle Peter.

This approach had to be abandoned, however, partly because of the impact of William Wrede's *Das Messias-Geheimnis in den Evangelien* (The Messianic Secret in the Gospels) in 1901,[1] and partly because of the rise of form criticism. Wrede showed that the scholars who approached the Gospel of Mark in a historicizing spirit had, in fact, to read into the text of the Gospel most of what they were getting from it. Far from being fundamentally a historical chronicle of the ministry of Jesus, the Gospel was rather the first chapter of a history of Christian doctrine; it was permeated throughout by early Christian dogmatic conceptions, especially that of the "messianic secret." Then, after Wrede came form criticism, which fundamentally altered our view of the Markan order and of the nature of the tradition in the Gospel.

Form Criticism

The form critics may be said to have affected the interpretation of the Gospel of Mark at three major points. They showed that the Markan outline was a construct of the Evangelist and not a reminiscence of the actual sequence of events in the ministry of Jesus. They demonstrated that the traditional material in the Gospel was essentially ahistorical. And they claimed that the Evangelist was to be understood as a collector, editor, and organizer of traditional material.

It was Karl Ludwig Schmidt who effectively destroyed the historicity of the Markan outline in his *Die Rahmen der Geschichte Jesu* (The Framework of the History of Jesus) in 1919.[2] He showed that the outline was a construct of the Evangelist himself, concluding his work with the sentence: "On the whole there is [in the Gospels] no life of Jesus in the sense of a developing story, as a chronological outline of the history of Jesus, but only isolated stories, pericopes, which have been provided with a framework." This judgment has been validated by fifty years of subsequent work on the Gospel, and today an important starting point in the interpretation of the Gospel is recognition of the fact that the actual ordering of events by the Evangelist himself is an important expression of his interpretation of Jesus and his story.

Form criticism, in general, saw the material in the Gospels as traditional, with a long history of interpretation and use in the early Christian communities and with much of it actually being created in those communities. Even where there might have been elements of historical reminiscence at the beginning, such elements were largely lost as the material was transmitted, interpreted, and used. This view of the Gospel material has gradually prevailed. Today it would be generally accepted, and the comparative realism of the narratives in Mark, or the naturalism of the presentation of Jesus, would not be considered an index of historicity.

If the form critics had a weakness, it was not in their view of the Markan outline or of the nature of the Gospel tradition but in their estimate of the literary activity of the Evangelist Mark. They were much more interested in the traditional material and its use in the early Christian communities than they were in the Evangelist and his literary activity. They regarded him as a collector and organizer of the traditional material, but responsible only for "relatively independent minor matters" (Martin Dibelius),[3] or as "not sufficiently master of his material to be able to venture on a systematic construction himself" (Rudolf Bultmann).[4] This comparative lack of interest in the Evangelist and his literary activity left a rather conspicuous gap for others to fill, and it was precisely at this point that progress in the interpretation of the Gospel was made. This brings us to R. H. Lightfoot in England and to Ernst Lohmeyer in Germany.

Lightfoot and Lohmeyer

R. H. Lightfoot was an English scholar who in the 1930s became dissatisfied with the historicizing approach to the Gospels prevalent in England and deliberately went to Germany to work with the form critics, especially Martin Dibelius. He became converted to the form-critical approach and returned to England to write a series of books advocating form criticism and taking the essential next step of investigating further the literary activity of the Evangelist Mark: *History and Interpretation in the Gospels, Locality and Doctrine in the Gospels,* and *The Gospel Message of St. Mark.*[5] Lightfoot investigated such things as Mark 1:1-13 and its function as the prologue to the Gospel; the Evangelist's presentation of John the Baptist and its christological purpose; the symbolic function of geographical references in the Gospel, especially the references to Galilee; the thematic concerns pursued by the Evangelist through various aspects of his work; and so on. He also developed a careful and generally convincing argument that the Evangelist intended to end his Gospel at 16:8, despite the barbarism of ending the book with a conjunction. In all of this he was anticipating the contemporary literary-critical approach to the Gospel.[6]

The climate of scholarship in England was generally hostile to form criticism and favorable to a historicizing approach to the Gospel of Mark. Lightfoot's work was not therefore as influential as it might otherwise have been. But he did influence a number of British scholars to approach the Gospel in a genuinely post–form-critical manner,[7] especially his own pupil D. E. Nineham, who wrote the Pelican commentary on the Gospel.[8]

In Germany, the first major approach to the Gospel in light of the findings of form criticism was Ernst Lohmeyer's commentary, *Das Evangelium des Markus* (The Gospel of Mark).[9] Lohmeyer seemed overwhelmed by the complexity of the Gospel material and unable to develop a systematic view of the literary activity of the Evangelist. He speaks of Mark following a geographical scheme, or of following theological or catechetical concerns. He sees the material as being organized according to major concerns, such as Jesus as teacher and healer, the disciples, the feeding stories, and so on. All of these observations are valid to a certain degree, but Lohmeyer does not succeed in integrating them. But his was the first commentary on the Gospel that paid particular attention to the Evangelist's literary activity, and the matter proved to be too complex for such a first attempt to be successful. Lohmeyer made important contributions, however, on individual points concerning the Evangelist's compositional techniques, for example his fondness for working with threefold units and for using related stories as brackets to hold together a larger unit of material, and so on.

REDACTION CRITICISM

Redaction Criticism (German: *Redaktionsgeschichte*) arose in Germany after World War II, much as form criticism had in fact risen after World War I. It came in the form of three decisive books: Günther Bornkamm, Gerhard Barth, and Heinz Joachim Held, *Überlieferung und Auslegung im Matthausevangelium* (1960; incorporating Bornkamm's pioneering essay on the stilling of the storm in Matthew, first published in 1947);[10] Hans Conzelmann, *Die Mitte der Zeit* (1954);[11] and Willi Marxsen, *Der Evangelist Markus: Studien zur Redaktionsgeschichte des Evangeliums* (1956).[12] As one can see, these books were concerned with Matthew, Luke-Acts, and Mark, respectively.

Redaction criticism returned to the form-critical concern for the Evangelist as the collector, editor (German: *Redaktor*), and organizer of traditional material; and it is concerned to isolate and to study the editorial process (*Redaktion*) carried out by the Evangelist. Bornkamm, Conzelmann, and Marxsen were all pupils of the pioneer form critic Rudolf Bultmann; and they considered themselves to be taking up and developing a hitherto comparatively neglected aspect of the form-critical method. In view of what was being done in England by Lightfoot and his followers, it is important to note that the German redaction critics were reluctant to treat the Evangelist fully as an author. They remained under the influence of the comparatively low view of the Evangelist and his literary activity held by Bultmann and Dibelius; and when Marxsen used the word "author" (*Schriftsteller*) with reference to the Evangelist Mark, he put it in inverted commas, as we shall see below.

In connection with Matthew and Luke-Acts, redaction criticism proved to be a most useful approach to interpretation. One could observe not only striking examples of the editing of individual pericopes, for example, Matthew's editing of the Markan account of the stilling of the storm to transform the miracle story into an allegory of the church, but also systematic editing, such as Matthew's studied avoidance of the verb "to teach" in connection with the disciples until the commissioning scene, or the constant de-emphasizing of eschatological references and the avoidance of soteriological ones in Mark by the author of Luke-Acts. Such observations proved enormously helpful in interpreting Matthew and Luke-Acts, but they were not possible in the case of

Mark, since in Mark we have access to no source that we could observe the Evangelist editing. In turning to Mark, therefore, Marxsen sought other ways of observing the Evangelist's use of traditional material.

Marxsen undertook four studies of the Gospel. In the first he took up Mark's editing and his use of the John the Baptist tradition, showing that Mark in general composes backwards—for example, the whole Gospel from the passion narrative—and that he composes the Baptist material "backwards" from Jesus, thereby making a christological point: "However the tradition at his disposal looked, Mark looses the Baptist from his historical context and sets him in front of Jesus by describing him, viewed from Jesus, as the forerunner of the Coming One."[13] Marxsen next turns to the geographical elements in the Gospel, noting particularly the important role played by the references to Galilee. He understood these references literally as geographical references and argued that Mark understood the story of Jesus as about to reach its climax in the parousia, which would take place in Galilee.[14] Marxsen then took up the term *euangelion,* arguing that the Evangelist uses it to indicate his purpose, which is essentially that of proclamation: "He [the Evangelist] is certainly a redactor, he works as an 'author,' and yet completely in the service of his theological point of view, of proclamation."[15] Marxsen finally turns to Mark 13 and, rejecting previous tendencies to break up the chapter and interpret it piecemeal, insists that "the whole—for Mark—must have a meaning." This meaning is that the end time has begun its course. Mark "transforms apocalyptic into eschatology"; so far as he is concerned "the *one* last act . . . has already begun and only the finale remains."[16] In accordance with his understanding of the references to Galilee as geographical, Marxsen understands Mark 13 as instructing the reader literally to flee to Galilee to await there the imminent parousia.[17]

In each of the four studies, Marxsen is concerned to bring out various aspects of the Evangelist's literary activity (editorial, compositional, thematic), and he is even prepared to use the word "author" in this connection, albeit in quotation marks. All of this activity, he argues consistently, is in the service of the Evangelist's theological understanding and purpose. In each study he goes on to discuss the further editing of the Markan material by Matthew and Luke, showing that this is always in the service of a theological understanding or purpose developed by Matthew or Luke in distinction from that of Mark. Marxsen's attention is directed to every aspect of the Evangelists' literary activity, although his emphasis is upon the strictly editorial; and for the critical discipline that concerned itself with this literary activity, he coined the term *Redaktionsgeschichte* (redaction history).

I was very much under the influence of Marxsen's usage when I defined redaction criticism as "concerned with studying the theological motivation of

an author as this is revealed in the collection, arrangement, editing, and mod-
ification of traditional material, and in the composition of new material or the
creation of new forms within the traditions of early Christianity."[18] However
valid this may be as a definition of redaction criticism, it is not the definition
of a critical method adequate to the interpretation of the Gospel of Mark
because it defines the literary activity of the Evangelist too narrowly. It does
not do justice to the full range of the literary activity of the Evangelist as
author; hence it cannot do justice to the full range of the text he has created. It
also suffers from a further drawback in that it concentrates attention entirely
upon the Evangelist—his literary activity and his theological motivation.
However exciting and productive that may be in a period of scholarship that is
just discovering the Evangelists as authors and theologians, it remains a fact
that this means that less than justice is being done to the text of the Gospel as
a coherent text with its own internal dynamics.

In retrospect one can see that after Marxsen what was needed for the further interpretation of the Gospel of Mark was the development of a critical
method that would, on the one hand, do justice to the full range of the Evangelist's literary activity, and, on the other hand, also move beyond concern for
authorial activity and theology to include a concern for the text of the Gospel
as a totality. In other words, it was necessary for redaction criticism to mutate
into a genuine literary criticism,[19] which it has done here in America.[20]

From Redaction Criticism to Literary Criticism

In this section I am concerned for the most part with recent American work
because it is primarily in America that this development has taken place.
Redaction criticism, however, can shade over into literary criticism in such a
way that no hard and fast distinctions are possible. Marxsen's work is in many
respects already literary-critical, and the same is true of Eduard Schweizer's
explicitly redaction-critical commentary, *Das Evangelium nach Markus*
(1967).[21] But the explicit discussion of the matter at the level of methodology,
and hence the self-conscious movement from the narrower redaction criticism to the broader literary criticism, has taken place in America.[22] The level of
conscious articulation of the methodological shift varies from critic to critic,
however, so I will discuss the matter in terms of literary-critical themes rather
than in terms of individual scholars.

Literary Genre

I will begin at the level of literary genre. To what literary genre does the Gospel
of Mark belong? Or, if one holds that Mark is himself the creator of the literary
genre "gospel" as I do: What literary model was the Evangelist following? There

have been several suggestions about this, but none have carried conviction. One is the aretalogy, a cycle of miracle stories exhibiting the power of a hero figure, possibly concluding with an account of his death as an apotheosis. Another is the Old Testament historical literature and the Book of Jonah. A third is the apocalyptic literature.[23] Via suggests that we should not look for a model but rather understand the Gospel of Mark as a product of a deep, generative structure of the human mind:

> Mark came to be written because the/a kerygma proclaiming, and the faith in, the death and resurrection of Jesus reverberated in the mind of Mark and activated the comic genre whose nucleus is also death and resurrection. . . . The story took the shape it did because the comic genre—a deep generative structure of the human mind—generated the Gospel of Mark as a performance text.[24]

Themes

A second feature of a literary-critical approach to Mark is a concern for the themes pursued by the Evangelist. It has become evident that Mark systematically pursues themes as he writes: the messianic secret, Christology and discipleship, a particular understanding of eschatology, the passion and the parousia, and others.[25] An approach to the Gospel by means of the thematic concerns of the Evangelist is a major feature of contemporary interpretation, and it is proving very fruitful.

Structure

A third feature of this approach to Mark is a concern for the structure of the Gospel. It is evident that the Evangelist is using isolated units of tradition with, at most, connected units of a very limited extent.[26] The ordering of the material and the overall structuring of the narrative is therefore particularly the work of the Evangelist, and the interpreter should pay particular attention to this structure, interpreting each part in terms of its function within the whole.[27] This is a concern of Schweizer's commentary on Mark, of my programmatic essay, "Towards an Interpretation of the Gospel of Mark," and of much other recent work. A concern for the structure at the various levels understood by structuralist criticism is the main feature of Dan Via's discussion of the Gospel in his *Kerygma and Comedy in the New Testament*.

Reports

Parallel to this concern for the structure of the Gospel is a concern for various distinctive features of the narrative. Among these are the summary reports that Mark regularly composes to link various parts of his narrative and to interpret it as it proceeds. Schmidt first called attention to these reports (German: *Sammelberichte*) in 1919, and they are still in the forefront of scholarly concern. Another such feature, akin to the summary reports, is the way in which certain narrative units, other than summary reports, serve a retrospective and a prospective function in the Gospel. For example, Mark 6:1-6a is retrospective and prospective of the "mighty works" of Jesus, of the "belief–unbelief" antithesis, of rejection and the passion. Similarly, 14:61 is retrospective of christological themes and prospective of the crucifixion as an enthronement of the centurian's confession, and of the parousia.[28]

Different Levels of Narrative

Another literary feature of the Gospel is the manner in which the narrative moves at several different levels. The Evangelist, for example, regularly addresses his readers directly out of his narrative. The reader is privy to the messianic secret, he is addressed directly by the Son of Man saying in Mark 2:10, and in the dialogue in 9:9-13; and his situation is mirrored in Mark 13. The narrative is not brought to an end so far as the reader is concerned, as the commissioning scene or the ascension bring the narratives of Matthew and Luke to an end for the readers of those Gospels, but rather the reader is left with the women at the empty tomb, awaiting the parousia. The investigation of the several levels at which the narrative of Mark moves is one of the strong points of Via's *Kerygma and Comedy*.

Characterization

A further feature of the contemporary literary-critical approach to the Gospel is Weeden's bold interpretation of Peter and the disciples as characters in a drama constructed by Mark in accordance with the rhetorical principles taught in the kind of school in which the Evangelist will have learned his Greek. This is an entirely justifiable procedure, and it makes *Mark—Traditions in Conflict* an important book, especially at the level of methodology in interpretation.[29]

Another important book at that level is Via's *Kerygma and Comedy*, which I have had occasion to mention at several points in this discussion. His book is important, in the first place, because it is specifically concerned with method in interpretation and has a very trenchant, if sometimes one-sided, discussion of various critical methods. Then, in the second place, the book is important because it introduces structuralist criticism as a critical method into the discussion of the interpretation of the Gospel of Mark. How important this method will eventually become, it is too soon to say; but it is certainly important for the would-be interpreter of Mark to wrestle with Via's book—and "wrestle" is the right word because not only is structuralism quite extraordinarily difficult to grasp, but also in this instance Via writes badly and argues clumsily. But some of his insights are compelling. In his hands, the Gospel becomes the homogeneous expression of a fundamental mindset, and both structure and various levels of the narrative of the Gospel are most meaningfully explored.[30]

One of the consequences of a literary-critical concern for the text of Mark as a totality is a concern for the meaning for Mark himself of the terms he uses and the incidents he narrates. We have long been accustomed to opening out the text of the Gospel and laying it against its background in early Christianity and the Hellenistic world. Our natural recourse has been to Kittel, Moulton and Milligan, or Strack-Billerbeck, or to any of the great collections of the Hellenistic materials. Now, however, we must also, as it were, roll up the text as a self-enclosed entity and ask what Mark understands by *euangelion,* what he intends by *paradidonai,* what the function of the transfiguration is for him, and so on. Of course we cannot do the one without the other, but the point is that we have to give proper attention to the second as well as to the first.

CONCLUSION

I will conclude by restating the point from which I began: The interpretation of the Gospel of Mark today requires a sophisticated, eclectic method of approach that can perhaps best be called literary criticism. This will include, of course, a deliberate attempt not to lose the gains of the old in an enthusiasm for the new. I am assuming that the concern for authorship, sources, and circumstances of writing characteristic of the older historical criticism will be carried over and taken up in the newer literary criticism.[31]

6

The Christology of Mark

Contemporary scholarly investigation of the Synoptic Gospels is dominated by redaction criticism, the key to which is the ability to distinguish material used by the Evangelist and the literary activity of the Evangelist in editing to determine the theology of the Evangelist.[1] The conviction is that one can do this by observing his literary activity in redaction and composition. In the cases of Matthew and Luke this has worked well, because we have a firm basis to work on as we observe their use of Mark and the Sayings Source Q.[2] In the past several years we have had real breakthroughs in our understanding of the theology of these two Evangelists, and redaction critics have established a firm basis for work in this area.[3] But in the case of the Gospel of Mark we have had no such basis for our work, and as yet we have had no such breakthrough in connection with the theology of the Second Evangelist (Mark).

METHODOLOGY

The problem in connection with Mark is one of method. Redaction criticism in this case is possible only to a limited extent, and it needs to be supplemented by other critical methods. As yet there is no scholarly consensus with regard to what particular blend of methods should be used in a historical investigation of the Gospel of Mark and the theology of the Second Evangelist. It is my purpose here to suggest such a blend and then to attempt to demonstrate the possibility inherent in the particular approach suggested by carrying out a sample investigation of an aspect of the theology of the Evangelist, namely, his Christology.

One aspect of our approach to the Gospel of Mark must be that of *redaction criticism* itself. Despite the difficulties inherent in the fact that we have none of Mark's sources, we must make a serious attempt to separate tradition from redaction and to determine the literary activity of the Evangelist. The main thrust of contemporary work on Mark is along these lines, and there are several ways of attempting to isolate Markan redaction. One is to use the literary factors of vocabulary and style. Examples of this approach would include the work of Eduard Schweizer and his pupil, Ulrich Luz,[4] or of Erich Grässer or Johannes Schreiber.[5] Another way is to pay careful attention to particular Markan concerns, such as the messianic secret, the geographical location Galilee (which in Mark is more than a geographical reference), or the use of Son of Man. A recent example of this approach is Etienne Trocmé's *The Formation of the Gospel according to Mark,* with its chapter "The Aversions Displayed by the Evangelist," and "The Causes Defended by Mark."[6] A third way is to pay careful attention to Markan compositional techniques: the use of intercalation, the fondness for threefold units, the practice of using related stories as parentheses to enclose a major unit, and so on. Ernst Lohmeyer in Germany and R. H. Lightfoot in England pioneered this approach during the 1930s, and it still remains a feature of the work of English scholars.[7] A fourth way is to attempt to isolate definite units of pre-Markan tradition and then to observe Mark's use of these units. Leander E. Keck did this with a cycle of miracle stories and its introduction,[8] and I attempted it with the Son of Man Christology.[9] In these and still other ways scholars attempt to identify Markan redaction of tradition and to proceed along the currently well-established lines of redaction criticism. But a major fact about Mark's Gospel is that it is a new creation—there was nothing like it before in early Christian literary history—and this leads to a second line of approach to the Gospel: the search for a model.

Prior to the writing of Mark there was no extended narrative gospel. There were connected units of tradition—a passion narrative, cycles of miracle stories, collections of sayings, collections of parables, an apocalyptic discourse, perhaps short collections of stories with a geographical center such as Capernaum or the Sea of Galilee, and so on—but no connected narrative beginning with John the Baptist and ending with the passion and/or resurrection (depending on one's view of the current ending of the Gospel at Mark 16:8). So Mark was creating *a new literary genre,* and the question is: What does the literary form he creates tell us about his purpose in writing? Or to put it another way: What literary model is he following? In the days when the Gospel of Mark was regarded as fundamentally a life of Jesus or a chronicle of the ministry of Jesus, this question did not arise. But with the widespread acceptance of the fact that the Gospel is neither a life nor a chronicle it does arise, and today it is being strenuously debated.

The most widely accepted view is that Mark's Gospel is "a passion narrative with an extended introduction"[10] and many contemporary interpretations of the Gospel proceed from this premise. This view does justice to Mark's theology of the cross, but it seems not to do justice to his eschatology. Another view being pressed at the moment is that Mark's Gospel is fundamentally an aretalogy, having grown out of a cycle of stories presenting Jesus as a divine man.[11] In conscious opposition to this latter view, Howard Kee argues that Mark is to be understood in apocalyptic terms, a view I would support.[12] This debate is only just getting underway, but it clearly is important. Our interpretation of Mark will depend very much upon any decision we make as to the model he is following—as to his purpose in writing as this is revealed in the literary form he is creating or imitating.

A consideration of the literary form of the Gospel of Mark leads to a third aspect of our approach to the work: an approach via the insights of general *literary criticism*. The Gospel of Mark is after all a literary text, and it should therefore be interpreted according to the canons of literary criticism. We should observe such things as the movement of the plot, the roles of the protagonists (especially, perhaps, Peter and the disciples), the literary structure of the total work, and so on. The Evangelist Mark may not be an author in the conscious and sophisticated sense of a William Shakespeare, Henry Fielding, or James Joyce; but he is an author, he has written a literary work, and he must be treated from the standpoint of literary criticism.

It is my contention that each of these three avenues of approach to the Evangelist Mark and his Gospel must be explored, and that the three approaches must be held in tension with one another. No one of them is the key to the whole, but together they offer us the opportunity to come close to Mark and his theology as redaction criticism has brought us to Matthew and Luke and their theologies.[13] As a *probe,* I turn to the question of the Christology of Mark.

Mark's Christology

Literary Criticism

Trial before the Sanhedrin

A consideration of the Christology of Mark can begin with a literary point: the importance to the Gospel of 14:53-71, the trial before the Sanhedrin and the denial of Peter. Here many of the themes that play a major role in the Gospel as a whole reach a climax. In v. 62, the messianic secret is unveiled, and in Peter's denial both the theme of the disciples' "hardness of heart" and Peter's role as leader of the disciples reach a tragic climax that Aristotle would have recognized. From a literary standpoint these scenes are climactic of what has gone before and preparatory of what is to come after—the account of the crucifixion.

We can reinforce the importance of these scenes to Mark by observing the amount of Markan literary activity in them. The trial scene (vv. 55-65) is intercalated between references to Peter in the courtyard (*aulē*; vv. 54, 66), a Markan composition and technique and itself bears strong evidence of Markan vocabulary and style.[14]

From the standpoint of Christology, the trial scene offers an important point. In v. 61, Jesus is addressed as Christ and Son of God; in v. 62 he accepts these designations and immediately interprets them by means of a use of Son of Man:

> "Are you the Christ, the Son of the Blessed?" Jesus said, "I am; and you will see the Son of Man sitting at the right hand of Power, and coming with the clouds of heaven" (vv. 61b-62).[15]

Caesarea Philippi

A very similar thing happens at Caesarea Philippi. Now the Caesarea Philippi pericope (Mark 8:27—9:1) is also very important from the standpoint of a literary-critical approach to the Gospel of Mark. As lives of Jesus without number testify, it is the watershed of Mark's literary composition. Furthermore, it also shows strong evidence of Markan literary activity.[16] At Caesarea Philippi Jesus is confessed as the Christ. He implicitly accepts this confession (not explicitly as in 14:62, because according to Mark's literary device it is not yet time for the messianic secret to be unveiled) and immediately goes on to interpret the designation in terms of a use of Son of Man:

> Peter answered him, "You are the Christ." . . . And he began to teach them that the Son of Man must suffer." (8:29b, 31a)

At two key points in his literary composition, therefore, Mark has Jesus interpret and give content to the titles "Christ" and "Son of God" by using "Son of Man."

Genre

Thus far we have approached the Christology of Mark by considering literary points—the role of the trial and denial and of the Caesarea Philippi pericope in the plot of the Gospel as a whole—and reinforcing those by considering the redaction-critical point of Markan literary activity in those pericopes. In other words, we have used the third and the first of the approaches advocated at the beginning of this paper. Now we will turn to the second: a consideration of the model Mark might be following and of what this will tell us of his purpose in writing. In this regard we have to admit at once that the discussion has not yet reached the point of a consensus as to the model for the Gospel as a whole, and therefore of an agreement as to Mark's overall purpose in writing.

But although we have no agreed model for the Gospel as a whole, scholarship does recognize models—and hence purposes—for certain aspects or parts of it. In particular it would be agreed that Mark inherits and uses the model of the Synoptic tradition itself. From its earliest days the Palestinian church used the form of sayings of Jesus and stories about him in preaching, in parenesis, in controversy and apologetic. A Son of Man saying exhorting to penitence, wisdom-type teaching to instruct in the essential preparation for the coming, controversies between the early believers and their Jewish brethren in the form of stories about Jesus and Pharisees, apologetic for the cross in the form of Jesus showing its divine necessity from the scriptures, all this and more is Mark's heritage and most immediate model. So we can say with confidence that the Gospel of Mark is in part *didactic narrative*. The form is a narrative of the ministry of Jesus; but the concerns are those of Mark and his church, and the purpose is directly to exhort, instruct, and inform Mark's readers.

Thus far we can go by general agreement. But we can go one step further, because there would also be general agreement that a major aspect of the Markan purpose is christological: He is concerned with correcting a false Christology prevalent in his church and to teach both a true Christology and its consequences for Christian discipleship. I have discussed this matter at some length elsewhere;[17] and, therefore, I may simply assert here the fact that Mark is concerned with correcting a false Christology, the point I argued earlier, and go on to make some further points in more detail.

Passion Predictions

An analysis of the literary structure of the Gospel reveals the importance of the three passion prediction units: Mark 8:31—9:1; 9:30-37; and 10:32-45. Each has exactly the same structure (prediction—misunderstanding—teaching), and each is a form of an interpretation of Peter's confession. The fact that there are three of them is certainly due to Mark's concern for threefold repetition. As has often been noted, they are part of the basic structure of the section of the Gospel (8:27—10:45) in which Mark presents his theology of the cross (*theologia crucis*). In these interpretations of Peter's confession, Mark is presenting his own passion-oriented Christology, using Son of Man, and then drawing out its consequences for Christian discipleship: in the first, the necessary preparedness Jesus exhibited; in the second, the necessity of servanthood; in the third, the climactic presentation of servanthood culminating in the ransom saying. At no point in the Gospel, except for the discourse in Mark 13, is Mark so clearly addressing and exhorting his own readers.

The dynamic use of the form of sayings and stories of Jesus in the Synoptic tradition has here become a literary convention, a convention that Mark establishes, develops, and adheres to strictly. The disciples set the stage by asking the questions or voicing the tendencies or opinions (and these are the questions, tendencies, and opinions present in Mark's church). The true Christology is then expressed by Jesus using Son of Man, and adhering to the convention, Son of Man is never found in Mark except on the lips of Jesus.[18] There is one possible exception to this, Mark 2:10. The abrupt change of subject and the tautologous repetition of the command to the paralytic indicate that the Son of Man saying may be an aside addressed by the Evangelist to his readers (see note 25 below). So a consideration of a possible model for an aspect of Mark's Gospel and of an aspect of his overall purpose leads us to a point already recognized: Mark uses Son of Man to correct and give content to a christological confession of Jesus as the Christ.

Correcting the "Divine Man" Christology

We can reach a similar point with regard to Son of God if we concentrate upon the first of our recommended approaches to the Gospel, the separation of redaction from tradition and the careful observation of the use made of tradition. Since Karl Ludwig Schmidt's epoch-making investigation of *Der Rahmen der Geschichte Jesu* (1919; The Framework of the History of Jesus), it has been generally recognized that Mark 3:7-12 is a Markan redactional summary and hence, more recently, that it, together with other summaries, is of great importance for a redaction-critical investigation of the Mark.[19] Mark 3:7-12 was further studied by Leander E. Keck who showed that it introduces a cycle of miracle stories in which Jesus is portrayed as a Hellenistic "divine man" (*theios anēr*; 3:7-12; 4:35—5:43; 6:31-52; 6:53-56) and Mark is concerned with playing down and correcting this understanding of Christology, as can be seen both from his redaction of the introduction and from his redaction of the cycle of stories themselves (especially the introduction of the secrecy motif).[20] The outlook of the original tradition was that of Jesus as a divine man, and Mark's own understanding of the Son of God category is sufficiently different from these stories to enable us to infer that he took them into his Gospel partly because they allowed him to present the divine sonship during Jesus' lifetime and partly because he wanted "to check and counterbalance this way of understanding Jesus' life and work."[21] Thus, on the basis of a redaction-critical investigation, Keck reached a conclusion similar to that which we have reached on other grounds.

Christ, Son of God, Son of Man

I am moving toward the point of claiming that the Christology of Mark may best be approached by assuming that he uses "Christ" and "Son of God" to establish rapport with his readers and then deliberately reinterprets and gives conceptual content to these titles by a use of "Son of Man," a designation that is not, properly speaking, a christological title but which to all intents and purposes becomes one as Mark uses it. Let me now approach this matter from the viewpoint of observing the occurrence of these three titles in Mark, paying attention to their place in the literary structure of the Gospel and to their relation with one another.

"Christ" is found in Mark at 1:1; 8:29; 9:41; 12:35; 13:21; 14:61; and 15:32. From the viewpoint of literary structure, three of these seven occurrences are comparatively unimportant:

9:41—with its parenetic use of "you bear the name of Christ"
13:21—a reference to false Christ is in the apocalyptic discourse[22]
15:32—the mocking at the cross.

A fourth, 12:35, where Christ is not the Son of David, is more difficult. It may be that Mark is here correcting a Son of David Christology, as elsewhere he corrects christologies associated with Christ and Son of God, but I must admit that as yet I have no firm opinion with regard to the function of the Son of David pericope in the Gospel of Mark. But the remaining three are all at key points in the Gospel:

1:1—the superscription defining the whole work as "the gospel of Jesus Christ"
8:29—the confession at Caesarea Philippi
14:61—the high priest's question at the trial.

In 1:1 the title is associated with Son of God in some textual traditions; in 8:29 and 14:61 it is immediately interpreted by a use of Son of Man.

In connection with my contention that Mark is concerned with correcting a false Christology prevalent in the church of his day, one should note how many of these references are to a false use of "Christ":

8:29—an immediate correction by a use of Son of Man
13:21—the false Christs
14:61—an immediate reinterpretation using Son of Man
15:32—the mocking.

Although Mark clearly intends the title to represent the full and proper Christian confession, especially in the central Caesarea Philippi pericope, in his

Gospel there is no correct human christological confession of Jesus until we come to the centurion in 15:39. The centurion uses Son of God, which is the most important title so far as Mark is concerned as he addresses his readers, as we shall see immediately below. It is not, however, the one by means of which he expresses his own Christology. He could not use it for that purpose because it could never have been made to bear the range of meaning he intended to fuse into his own Christology. The correct confession by the centurion is possible because by 15:39 the literary process of correcting the Christology held by Mark's readers is complete, having been completed by Jesus' response to the high priest's question at the trial.

"Son of God" (or its equivalent) is to be found in Mark six or seven times, always at places important to the Gospel as a whole. According to some textual traditions it is part of the superscription in 1:1.[23] Then it occurs at each of the places in the Gospel where cosmic phenomena (heavens opening, or the like) indicate a revelatory moment according to the conventions of the first century C.E.:

1:11—the baptism
9:7—the transfiguration.

Then it occurs twice on the lips of demons, creatures whose supernatural origin would indicate supernatural knowledge in the world in which Mark lived and for which he wrote:

3:11—unclean spirits, in redactional summary
5:7—Gerasene demoniac.

Finally, it is linked with "Christ":

14:61—the high priest's question
15:39—centurion's confession.

The centurion's confession is clearly for Mark a climactic moment.

It can be seen that neither "Christ" nor "Son of God" is especially frequent in Mark, but that the former is found at key moments in the narrative and that every occurrence of the latter is significant. "Son of Man" occurs much more frequently than either, a total of fourteen times: Mark 2:10; 2:28; 8:31; 8:38; 9:9; 9:12; 9:31; 10:33; 10:45; 13:26; 14:21 (2x); 14:41; 14:62. The sheer frequency of occurrence of this title indicates its importance for Mark; but at the same time it presents problems to the interpreter, for the fact is that the usage does not immediately appear to be homogeneous. A comparatively crude division is that into three:

Present authority: 2:10; 2:28
Apocalyptic: 8:38; 13:26; 14:62
Suffering: 8:31; 9:12; 9:31; 10:33; 10:45; 14:21 (2x); 14:41.

But that leaves one unaccounted for, 9:9, and the third group is not really a group at all. To say the very least, the predictions, 8:31; 9:31; 10:33, have to be separated from the rest as having an internal cohesiveness of their own. At the same time it is possible to account for each occurrence in terms of inherited tradition, Markan development of that tradition, and creation of new tradition, and by doing this to reach the heart of the Christology of Mark. To this task we now turn.

We will begin with Mark 9:9, the redactional command to secrecy "until the Son of Man be risen from the dead." It would be generally acknowledged that this is Markan redaction and, equally, that it is important to an understanding of the secret and of the Markan purpose altogether. In the Gospel of Mark the transfiguration is proleptic of the parousia;[24] and this saying directs Mark's readers to the post-resurrection pre-parousia situation in which they stand and to which Mark is directing the teaching he puts on the lips of Jesus. That the saying uses Son of Man is due in part to the fact that it is Mark's own designation of Jesus and also probably in part to the proximity of the predictions of the passion and resurrection. In any case, the saying is readily explicable and understandable as a Markan hint to his readers as to his own understanding of his purpose in writing.

Let us take next the two references to the Son of Man's authority on earth in the present of the ministry of Jesus, "the Son of Man has authority on earth to forgive sins" (2:10), and "the Son of Man is Lord even of the Sabbath (2:28). I have argued elsewhere that these represent a particularly Markan development of a tendency at work in the Synoptic traditions, and I would repeat that here.[25] Only in Mark and in dependence on Mark is *exousia* ("authority") used of the earthly ministry of Jesus in the Synoptic Gospels. And from a literary standpoint these two references to the Son of Man stand dramatically in the section of the Gospel in which the authority of Jesus in word and deed is being thematically presented (1:16—3:6). There are no further references to the Son of Man until it begins to play its dominant role in the central interpretative section of the Gospel (8:27—10:45). The movement toward the view of Jesus' earthly ministry as already exhibiting his full authority is to be found in the Synoptic tradition, for example, Matt 8:9 (and par.). But it is Mark who first takes the step of using *exousia* of that earthly ministry and linking it with Son of Man. Moreover, there is real literary artistry in the two uses of Son of Man in the first major section of the Gospel that are followed by two uses of Son of God in the second (Mark 3:11 and 5:7 in the section 3:7—6:6a). The two are thereby established as equivalent designations for Jesus in his full authority, and the

way is prepared for the interpretation of the latter in terms of the former that is
a fundamental part of Mark's christological concern. The use of Son of Man in
2:10 and 2:28, therefore, fits smoothly into Mark's overall concern.

The three uses of Son of Man in apocalyptic context in Mark (8:38; 13:26;
14:62) present no problems. I have discussed them all at some length elsewhere;[26] and I may simply reiterate the conclusion that 8:38 is a Markan redaction of a "sentence of holy law" (Käsemann) just as that now found in Luke
12:8-9 (and par.); Mark 13:26 is an early Christian apocalyptic promise; and
14:62 a product of early Christian midrash-pesher use of the Old Testament.[27]
What we have here is the use by Mark of early Christian tradition: 8:38 juxta-
poses with 8:31 in the Caesarea Philippi pericope, and so provides the basis for
the full development of Mark's Son of Man Christology in 8:27—10:45, a point
to which we shall be returning; 13:26 sounds a keynote in the apocalyptic discourse by means of which Mark seeks to prepare his readers directly for the
requirements of their pre-parousia situation; and 14:62 is the climactic element in Mark's christological statement, fittingly so since it comes in the trial
scene that is a climax of Mark's literary activity, as I argued above. For his own
purpose, Mark is here mining and using elements from the early and well-
established apocalyptic Son of Man Christology of the church.

Six Difficult Passages
The real problems arise in connection with the remaining sayings: 9:12b; 10:45;
14:21, 41; and the predictions in 8:31; 9:31; and 10:33-34. But the problems here
lie in the area of determining the element of Markan literary activity in the
composition of these sayings;[28] their use in the overall literary structure of the
Gospel fits the pattern of the Markan use of Son of Man that I would claim is
beginning to emerge.

Mark 9:12b
Mark 9:12b, where the Son of Man is to experience "many sufferings and
treated with contempt" (*polla pathē kai exoudenēthē*), shatters the tight-knit
structure of 9:9-13 so obviously that many commentators have argued that it is
a post-Markan gloss that crept early into the text of the Gospel, and I can only
agree. It can and indeed must be ignored so far as the use of Son of Man by
Mark is concerned.

Mark 10:45
Mark 10:45 is a saying with a complex history. In the first place, Mark probably
inherited it in a Eucharistic setting, for the parallel section in Luke (22:24-27)
does have such a setting, and it is clear that Mark has extensively rearranged
his traditional material, especially in the carefully constructed central section
of his Gospel: 8:22—10:52. Further, Lohse has argued convincingly that both

Mark 10:45 and the "I am among you as one who serves" of Luke 22:27 have independent histories in the tradition of the church, the former in a more Semitic and the latter in a more Hellenistic area.[29] If that is the case then the question is which is the more original, the form using Son of Man or that using the first person singular. In general it can be shown that Luke 22:24-27 with its concern for church order is somewhat later than Mark 10:42-45,[30] and in any case where we have tradition in both a more Semitic and a more Hellenistic form the probability is that the former is earlier than the latter, since the church did, in fact, begin as a sect within Palestinian Judaism and move into the Hellenistic world by means of a Hellenistic Jewish Christian mission. So the balance of the probability is that the Son of Man is the more original and that the I-saying was formed from it. In that case the original saying was in some such form as, "The Son of Man came to seek and to save the lost" (Luke 19:10; see Matt 19:11). Is it perhaps possible that both these sayings have a common point of origin in a moment of solemn reflection at a very early Christian Eucharist? Be that as it may, the verbal parallel with Luke 22:27 and the sense parallel with Luke 19:10 indicate that at one time Mark 10:45a existed as a complete saying and that the ransom clause was added as a gloss.[31] This glossing certainly took place in the Semitic language area of the tradition of the church and very probably in a Eucharistic setting. Mark 10:45b has a strongly Semitic cast, and it and the Eucharistic word (Mark 14:24) are the only allusions to Isaiah 53 that can be definitely located in the Semitic language area of the tradition of the church. It is very probable therefore that they have a common original setting.

I have discussed the origin of Mark 10:45 at some length because of its intrinsic interest. But for our immediate purpose the origin of the saying is less important than the use to which Mark puts it, and that is clear enough. He uses it to climax the threefold teaching on discipleship in the passion prediction units and in this way to link that teaching decisively to the Son of Man Christology, which for him is its essential basis.

Mark 14:21, 41

In 14:21, 41 we have an apologetic use of Son of Man with the verb *paradidonai*, whereby the passion of Jesus is summarized by the verb—which means to "betray," "deliver up"—and the stress is on the divine necessity for the passion. The link between Son of Man and the verb (*para*)*didonai* in connection with the passion is pre-Markan,[32] and in that sense Mark 14:21, 41 are traditional, whatever the actual history of the Gethsemane material may be in the Synoptic tradition and in Mark's Gospel. As they stand, these Son of Man sayings are Markan echoes of traditional early Christian passion apologetic. All passion narratives in the New Testament are saturated with such notes, including Mark's.

Mark 8:31; 9:31; and 10:33-34

The real problem with regard to Markan composition is presented by the predictions of the passion and resurrection in 8:31; 9:31; and 10:33-34. The three most recent discussions of this matter, all from an avowedly redaction-critical standpoint, show a steady progression toward recognition of Markan literary activity: H. E. Tödt thought all three were traditional. Ferdinand Hahn thought that the first and second were traditional, the third being Markan. And Georg Strecker thought that the first was traditional, the second and third being Markan.[33] It is my personal conviction that all three have been composed by Mark, who has mined their constituent parts from the (*para*)*didonai* tradition and the passion apologetic of earliest Christianity.[34] Be that as it may, the use of the predictions by Mark is not in dispute. He uses them to develop the passion-oriented element of his own Christology and to form the basis for the consequent teaching on the essential nature of discipleship that follows each of them in the stereotyped pattern of the three passion-prediction units (8:31; 9:31; and 10:33-34).

CONCLUSION

The position with regard to the Son of Man Christology in the tradition prior to Mark and the Markan use of that tradition now becomes clear. Prior to Mark there are three uses of Son of Man in the tradition:

- in an apocalyptic context
- in reflection upon the significance of Jesus' ministry, probably in a Eucharistic setting
- with (*para*)*didonai* in apologetic for the passion.

From these beginnings Mark develops the threefold emphasis that is characteristic of his Gospel—apocalyptic, authority in the present, and suffering. And all the references to Son of Man in the Gospel become explicable on the basis of this hypothesis of inherited tradition and Markan development of it. Beyond this, an approach to the Gospel along the three avenues of redaction criticism, the question of model or purpose, and general literary criticism shows that Mark is using Son of Man to express his own Christology and that he uses Christ and Son of God to establish rapport with readers, and Son of Man to interpret and give content to those titles. It is not the claim of this paper that these conclusions are new—on the contrary, they would generally be accepted by the world of scholarship. But it is the claim of the paper that the fact that they can be reached by the approach suggested validates that approach and suggests a similar approach to other aspects of the Markan theology and purpose.

7

Jesus and the Theology
of the New Testament

THREE MAJOR PROBLEMS

New Testament as a Theological Entity

I begin with a categorical statement: the academic study of the theology of
the New Testament is today in a state of disarray. There are, to be specific,
three major problems we have to face, problems to which no immediate and
convincing answer is readily to be found. In the first place there is the problem as to whether the New Testament is itself a meaningful theological entity.
Historically speaking, the New Testament represents but a selection from the
literature produced by the early Christian communities down to about 140
C.E., and the question is whether this act of selection is to be held to be significant or not. Historical study has revealed all the ambiguities within the
process that led to the formation of the canon, and comparative studies have
shown that not all the decisions made in the fourth Christian century with
regard to inclusion in or exclusion from the canon would be ratified today. So
do we attempt to write a "theology of the New Testament," or do we go for a
"history of the religion of early Christianity": that is the first of the problems
we have to face.

Theology or Theologies of the New Testament

If we decide, for whatever reason, to write a theology of the New Testament,
then a second problem immediately arises. The problem, namely, as to
whether we can find *a* theology of the New Testament or whether we are going
to have to review *all* the *theologies within* the New Testament. Again it is historical study that has revealed the problem because historical study has
revealed the manifold diversity of the theologies within the New Testament. In
the last ten years or so this problem has become more acute than ever as we

have added the theologies of the Synoptic Evangelists to those of Paul, John, and the literature of emergent Catholicism. W. G. Kümmel recently published a *Theology of the New Testament according to Its Major Witnesses*.[1] I must admit that I can no longer see how a scholar can treat Paul and John as "major witnesses" to the theology of the New Testament over against emergent Catholicism on the one hand or Mark, Matthew, and the author of Luke-Acts on the other. Leaving aside Jesus for the moment, there are at least five major theological viewpoints expressed directly in the New Testament, and if we add the "letter" to the Hebrews, the deutero-Pauline Colossians and Ephesians, and the early Christian apocalyptic Ernst Käsemann has taught us to recognize—as we almost certainly should—then those five rapidly become eight. The problem of the unity within the diversity is becoming ever more acute.

The Historical Jesus

I have just said, "leaving aside Jesus for the moment," but of course one cannot leave Jesus aside, even for a moment, and therein lies one of the major problems in connection with the theology of the New Testament, the so-called question of the historical Jesus. On the one hand, Rudolf Bultmann begins his *Theology of the New Testament* by roundly declaring that "the message of Jesus is a presupposition for the theology of the New Testament rather than a part of that theology itself," and in this he is supported by his pupil Hans Conzelmann, who insists that "the 'historical Jesus' is not a theme within the theology of the New Testament."[2] In stark and quite deliberate contrast, both Joachim Jeremias and Leonhard Goppelt begin projected two-volume theologies of the New Testament with the first volume devoted entirely to the historical Jesus, while Kümmel views Jesus as one of the three main witnesses to the theology of the New Testament, as we have just seen.[3] Clearly there is a problem here in urgent need of further discussion.

ADDRESSING THE THREE MAJOR PROBLEMS

Canon, History, and Theology

I may now repeat my opening statement: the academic study of the theology of the New Testament is today in a state of disarray. But since it is in disarray, in my view, because of the three problems I have identified, I may now go further and approach these three problems, beginning with the problem of the canon and with therefore the choice between attempting a theology of the New Testament or a history of the religion of early Christianity. Let me say at once that I would welcome a history of the religion of early Christianity and that I would gladly join in the enterprise of writing such a history. At the same time, however, the fact remains that the New Testament is an entity that, as an entity, has played and does play an enormous role in Christian history, and I am not prepared to dissolve it into something else without much stronger grounds than the historical ambiguities of the process of the formation of the canon and the odd nature of the choices made from the literature of emergent Catholicism. A history of the religion of early Christianity would be most welcome, but from the standpoint of the Christian communities a theology of the New Testament is an urgent need.

Unity and Diversity

That brings me to the second problem, the problem of theological unity and diversity within the New Testament, and the question whether we can write a theology of the New Testament or only compile a collection of the theologies within the New Testament. This problem has become more acute, as I indicated earlier, because of our increasing ability to identify such theologies. I must say at once that I view the investigation of the theologies within the New Testament as I view the writing of a history of the religion of early Christianity: it is a legitimate scholarly enterprise and one to be welcomed warmly. Indeed I have spent no small part of the last few years working on the theology of the evangelist Mark and encouraging others to work on that theology and on the theologies of the evangelist Matthew and of the author of Luke-Acts. Such work contributes to the theology of the New Testament in that it helps us to appreciate the richness—and the extent!—of the diversities among the theologies within the New Testament, but if we are to achieve a theology of the New Testament, we must first find a motif, a theme, a factor by means of which we can identify a unity within the diversity. I turn, then, to a discussion of the possibility of finding such a motif, theme, or factor.

It is well known that in recent Protestant scholarship—I cannot, unfortunately, claim the competence to discuss recent Roman Catholic scholarship in this connection—*two* such unifying factors have been proposed: the kerygma of the early Christian communities and the historical Jesus. Bultmann builds his theology of the New Testament around the factor of the kerygma, and in this he is followed by his pupil Conzelmann. Another pupil, Herbert Braun, has a reductionist variation on this theme in which a common anthropology is the unifying factor. Jeremias, on the other hand, builds his theology of the New Testament around the factor of Jesus, the historical Jesus, the Jesus known to historical-critical investigation, and in this he is followed by Goppelt. The question of the historical Jesus and the theology of the New Testament is the third of the problems that I am calling to your attention as well as the main theme of this essay, and I shall be turning to it immediately below. Let me, then, say something now about the kerygma as the unifying factor of the theology of the New Testament, discussing the issue specifically in connection with Bultmann's work.

Bultmann's understanding of the theology of the New Testament is too well known for me to need to do more than to remind you of some of its main features. He views Jesus and his message as an essential presupposition, but only a presupposition, of the theology of the New Testament, and he puts all the emphasis on the kerygma of the Church. Where Jesus had proclaimed the radical demand of God, the early Church proclaimed the future (not the second, but the future) coming of Jesus as the radical demand of God. The earliest Church regarded itself as the eschatological congregation, and in this self-understanding there lay the seeds for the understanding of the *past* of Jesus, his ministry, death, and resurrection, as also being eschatological occurrence.

In "the Hellenistic Church aside from Paul," this kerygma is developed further. The monotheism necessary in the Hellenistic world is added, and the basic proclamation becomes one of monotheism, repentance, and eschatological judgment. There develops, further, an emphasis on the resurrection of Jesus. The total proclamation is understood as *euangelion* (good news) and its acceptance as *pistis* (faith). The Christian Church is at this stage a cult within Hellenistic religiosity, and it worships Jesus as Lord and Son of God and develops the sacraments of baptism and Eucharist according to essentially Hellenistic models.

This is the kerygma that Paul inherits, and he in turn develops and interprets it so that it becomes, for the first time, a full-fledged theology. Bultmann's presentation of the theology of Paul is justly famous. Independently of Paul, John takes up, develops, and interprets the kerygma so that again we have a full-fledged theology. And Bultmann waxes almost as eloquent and enthusiastic over the Johannine theology as he does over the Pauline.

The same cannot be said, however, about Bultmann's presentation of "the development toward the ancient Church," the last major section of his theology of the New Testament. He describes what I have called "emergent Catholicism" carefully and at length, but over and over again he calls attention to differences from Paul and from John, invariably negatively. So far as Bultmann is concerned, the theology of the New Testament peaks in the theologies of Paul and John: what came before is preparation; what comes after is an anticlimax.

For the past twenty years (1955–75) Bultmann dominated the academic study of the theology of the New Testament, and one can see why this has been the case. He has a global understanding of the New Testament in which full justice is done to both historical and theological considerations. His understanding of a development from the proclamation of the earliest Christian communities, both primitive Palestinian and Hellenistic, to the theologies of Paul and John and on to the literature of emergent Catholicism is obviously correct in its broad outline, and subsequent research has only developed and modified it in its details. Moreover his emphasis on the kerygma as the unifying factor is, at first sight, persuasive, especially if one emphasizes the Pauline letters and the pre-Pauline elements identified in them on form-critical grounds, as Bultmann does. The one element in the whole that might give one reason for hesitation is the comparative denigration of the literature of emergent Catholicism. But this would not disturb his fellow Lutherans, while the rest of us would tend to write it off as a Lutheran prejudice. Yet it is in fact an indication of the fatal flaw in Bultmann's whole enterprise in attempting to write a theology of the New Testament. He has not achieved a theology of the New Testament at all, but only a theology of Paul and John. It is simply not the case that everything before Paul and John is preparation for them and that everything after them is a falling away from their achievements. Let me hasten to add that this negative judgment of Bultmann's *Theology of the New Testament* is not an attempt to belittle his attainment. His work is and will remain the necessary starting point for any approach to the theology of the New Testament for the foreseeable future. But in the last twenty years we have reached, on the one hand, an understanding of early Christian apocalyptic and, on the other hand, an understanding of the theologies of the Synoptic Evangelists that call for a radical rethinking of Bultmann's understanding of the theology of the New Testament. But before I discuss these things in any detail, let me turn to the third question, the question of the historical Jesus.

Anyone who has read, or even looked at, my *New Testament: An Introduction* knows that I, a pupil of Joachim Jeremias, have come to share Bultmann's view of Jesus, the historical Jesus, as the presupposition of the New Testament. In that book I explicitly designate Jesus as "the presupposition of the New Testament," and I reserve my discussion of him until the twelfth and last chapter.[4] Moreover, I acknowledge in the first chapter that this is a direct consequence of years of wrestling with the opening sentence of Bultmann's *Theology of the New Testament,* a sentence that I first rejected but that I now thoroughly accept. The historical Jesus is a presupposition of the theology of the New Testament and as such essential to the New Testament and its theology, but the Jesus who plays such an important role in the New Testament, especially in the Synoptic Gospels, is simply not the historical Jesus. He is a "faith image" of Jesus, a "perspectival image" of Jesus, an image being reinterpreted by the Synoptic Evangelists in accordance with their own theology perspectives.

Jesus as Faith Image

I have now reached the central concern of this essay, and I must proceed with some care. Let me begin at this point by attempting to clarify what I mean by a faith image of Jesus or by a perspectival image of him. The phrase "faith image" is my own, and I first developed it in the discussion of the question of the historical Jesus I offered in the fifth chapter of my *Rediscovering the Teaching of Jesus*. The phrase "perspectival image" is Van A. Harvey's, developed by him in his book *The Historian and the Believer.*[5] Completely independently of each other we reached a similar understanding of the question of the historical Jesus, an understanding that may be expressed as follows. At the beginning of the stream of tradition that eventually forms the basis for the Gospels there stands the historical Jesus, his message and his ministry, the impact he made on his followers, and the memories of him that lived on after his death. With the coming of belief in his resurrection and the growing sense of his presence through his spirit in the experience of the believer and in the life of the believing community, the memory image of Jesus becomes transformed into the faith or perspectival image, an image in which the memory of the historical Jesus plays only a part, however important that part may be. It must always be remembered that it is Jesus *Christ* who is the concern of the New Testament and of Christian faith. As Erich Grässer puts the matter: *Jesus Christ,* not the "man from Nazareth," is the concern and content of faith. "Jesus" expresses what he *was* yesterday; "Christ" expresses what he *is,* the same today and forever.[6] The New Testament is always concerned with this image of Jesus, this mixture of "was" and "is." In light of the New Testament one cannot justify an insistence on either the "was" or the "is" to the exclusion of the other. From the perspective of the New Testament it is as nonsensical to ground faith in the historical Jesus as it is to deny that historical knowledge of Jesus is of any concern to faith. The concern of faith is the faith or perspectival image of Jesus, and this image began with historical reminiscence of Jesus, "wie er eigentlich *gewesen ist*" (as he actually had been), and this image continues to be informed by such historical knowledge of Jesus as we are able to recover from our sources. At the same time, however, this image of Jesus is essentially the image mediated to us by what would be called "the means of grace" in the tradition from which I came and "the sacraments" in other traditions. It is essentially the image of the Jesus we experience *in* faith, Jesus "wie er eigentlich *ist*" (as he actually is). Of course, the real problem then becomes the balance or tension between these two, and both Van Harvey and I discussed that problem at length. Today I may simply refer you to those discussions. My intention in this essay is only to argue that the concern of faith, and of the theology of the New Testament, is with the faith image of Jesus, not with the historical Jesus.

ASPECTS OF A NEW TESTAMENT THEOLOGY

It is for this reason that I have felt compelled to abandon the viewpoint of my own teacher, Joachim Jeremias. I could not devote the first volume of a two-volume *Theology of the New Testament* to the historical Jesus and his message because the historical Jesus does not play so proportionately large a role in the New Testament itself. The Jesus of the New Testament is the Jesus Christ of Christian faith; he is the Jesus of the faith or perspectival image of Christian experience. If I can no longer follow Jeremias, then I certainly cannot follow Goppelt or Kümmel; I must begin where this New Testament begins, with the Jesus Christ who is always the Jesus of Christian experience, a blend of the Jesus who was and of the Christ who is.

If you will allow me this as my starting point, then let me now sketch some of the aspects of the theology of the New Testament that follow from it, paying special attention to those elements within the New Testament that I see as creating difficulties for Bultmann's understanding of that theology, early Christian apocalyptic and the theologies developed by the Synoptic Evangelists. In what follows I shall be building on the work I presented in my *Introduction*. I shall not reargue here points I made there but rather assume them and go on to develop their significance for an understanding of the theology of the New Testament.

Apocalyptic

The Christian movement began as an apocalyptic sect within ancient Judaism. It differed from other Jewish apocalyptic sects in that it proclaimed *Jesus* as the one who was to come as Son of Man and apocalyptic redeemer. It differed from Jesus in that, where Jesus had proclaimed the Kingdom of God as eschatological event, it proclaimed the future coming of Jesus as eschatological event. But its most distinctive feature was a third, namely, that it believed that the Jesus who was to come as Son of Man had already appeared proleptically to some of his followers in his apocalyptic splendor and that his spirit was already at work in the community of those who believed in him. I should perhaps emphasize the fact that I am convinced that the experience of the Resurrection and of the Spirit in earliest Christianity was not understood as an experience of the earthly Jesus of the past but as a proleptic experience of the glorified Jesus of the future.

Theologically speaking, the earliest Christian communities were thoroughly at home in the world of Jewish apocalyptic. Their models were the models of Jewish apocalyptic, and they interpreted Jesus and their own experience of him in terms of Jewish sacred texts in a manner now known to us from the Qumran commentaries (*pesharim*). These Christian communities were sociologically and self-consciously part of the wider Jewish community. They accepted the Jewish foundation myths; their rituals were Jewish rituals; their forms of piety were Jewish; their interpretation of Jesus and their own experience were built on Jewish models, with the aid of Jewish texts interpreted according to a Jewish hermeneutics. Their fundamental theological model was the model of Jewish apocalyptic, and when they used material derived from the historical Jesus, they used it in the service of a proclamation and a theology that they did not derive from Jesus himself.

That last point is to my mind a crucial point. Early Christian apocalyptic derived its theological mode not from Jesus but from the world of Jewish apocalyptic. When the earliest Christian communities took up and reused the message of Jesus concerning the Kingdom of God, as they did, then they did so in the service of their theological understanding of the future coming of Jesus as Son of Man as eschatological event. In *Jesus and the Language of the Kingdom*, I have argued in detail that "Kingdom of God" is, on the lips of Jesus, a symbol, and a symbol that functions by evoking a myth, the myth of God active within the history of his people on their behalf.[7] This myth was fully accepted by both Jesus and his hearers, and Jesus was able to use the symbol dramatically and effectively to mediate to his hearers the experience of God as King by means of symbolic acts and the use of symbolic language. Early Christian apocalyptic, however, had a very different version of the myth of God as King from that which Jesus held. It held the version developed in Jewish apocalyptic whereby the experience of God as King is not mediated in the present by symbolic acts and symbolic language but awaited in the future when it will be known in terms of concrete historical events. Theologically speaking, there is a world of difference between these two. Let us illustrate the difference quite concretely by referring you to Luke 17:20-24.

In Luke 17:20-21 we have a genuine saying of Jesus:

> The Kingdom of God is not coming with signs to be observed, nor will they say, "Lo, here it is!" or "There!" for behold the Kingdom of God is in the midst of you.

Whatever else that most difficult saying may be held to mean, it certainly means that the activity of God as King is something that the hearers of Jesus may expect to know as an existential and experiential reality. In the tradition represented by Luke 17:20-24, however, it has been reinterpreted by means of a Son of Man saying to give it a quite different meaning, and the Son of Man saying is certainly a product of early Christian apocalyptic. It follows the regular literary device of introducing reinterpretation as private teaching to the disciples, and it is linked to the genuine, dominical saying by means of the catchwords "Lo, here!" and "Lo, there!"

> The days are coming when you will desire to see one of the days of the Son of Man; and you will not see it. And they will say to you, 'Lo, there!' or 'Lo, here!' Do not go, do not follow them. For as the lightning flashes

and lights up the sky from one side to the other, so will the Son of Man be in his day. (Luke 17:22-24)

There are two major differences between the saying of Jesus and this reinterpretation of it in early Christian apocalyptic. The first is that not all signs are denied, but only readily identifiable ones. In *Jesus and the Language of the Kingdom,* I discuss this matter at length, with the aid of recent literary critical and philosophical work on the nature and function of signs and symbols, and I attempt to show that the difference between Jesus and early Christian apocalyptic on the nature and function of signs is very great indeed and indicative of a major difference in the understanding of the nature and function of religious language. Briefly summarized, the difference is that Jesus used symbolic language in such a way that the symbols were "tensive" (Wheelwright) or "true" (Ricoeur) symbols, and the language itself mediated the reality to which it referred. Early Christian apocalyptic, however, for the most part used symbolic language in such a way that the symbols were "steno" symbols (Wheelwright) or "signs" rather than true symbols (Ricoeur), and it did not mediate the reality to which it referred but rather pointed to a future mediation of that reality in the coming of Jesus as Son of Man. I regard this as a distinction of enormous theological significance, and I base it on a book-length discussion of Jesus and the language of the Kingdom. Obviously I cannot repeat that discussion here but only point to the conclusion I am drawing from it. The *language* of Jesus, and the fact that it was the language of *Jesus,* mediated to his hearers the existential and experiential reality of God as King. The language of early Christian apocalyptic, on the other hand, claims that the existential and experiential reality of God as King will be mediated to the believer at the moment in the future when Jesus comes as Son of Man.

The second major difference between the dominical saying in Luke 17:20-21 and its early Christian apocalyptic reinterpretation in vv. 22-24 is the obvious and often noted one. Verses 20-21 proclaims the Kingdom of God as eschatological event; vv. 22-24 proclaims the future coming of Jesus as eschatological event. This has often been pointed out, and as far as I know it has not been seriously disputed. I therefore need do no more than mention it and call attention to the fact that it reinforces the first point I made in this connection, a point that, so far as I know, is new and has not been made before.

I now need to pause for a moment in order to make clear the difference between the views I am presenting here and those presented by Bultmann in *Theology of the New Testament.* Bultmann saw Jesus as himself using the whole Jewish apocalyptic mythology in the service of a particular understanding of existence, an understanding of existence in which every hour is the last hour for the man who stands in the crisis of decision before God. Now

I challenge this, so far as the use by Jesus of Jewish apocalyptic symbols is concerned. In my view, Jesus used the apocalyptic symbols as tensive symbols, whereas in Jewish apocalyptic they are, for the most part, steno symbols. By his use of the symbolic language and by symbolic acts Jesus mediated to certain of his contemporaries a direct experience of God as King, whereas Jewish apocalyptic, and, for that matter, later Christian apocalyptic also, used the symbolic language in preparation for an experience of God as King in the future. There are, historically speaking, major differences between Jesus' use of the language of the Kingdom and the use of that language in Jewish apocalyptic, as there are major differences between Jesus' use of the language of the Kingdom and the use of the language of the coming of the Son of Man in early Christian apocalyptic.

Bultmann was not in a position to see these differences, and, further, his concern was mainly to achieve an interpretation of the message of Jesus for the twentieth century. He was too quick in his movement from what it *said* to what it *says*. He accepted an incorrect understanding of the use by Jesus of apocalyptic symbolism—which he generally and inaccurately called mythology rather than symbolism—and he moved immediately to "demythologize" that use as representing an understanding of existence that could be translated into the twentieth century. When I discussed this matter earlier in my Society of Biblical Literature presidential address on "Eschatology and Hermeneutics," I agreed that in the end I too would probably reach a position close to Bultmann's as far as the interpretation of the message of Jesus into the twentieth century was concerned.[8] But I would reach it on the basis of an understanding and interpretation of Jesus' use of symbolic language, not on the basis of a hermeneutics of demythologizing, which in this instance is too crude a hermeneutical method.

A second difference between Bultmann's views and those that I am presenting here is occasioned by the fact that Bultmann wrote before the work on early Christian apocalyptic, done above all by Ernst Käsemann, and before the work on the theology of Q, begun by Heinz Eduard Tödt and brought to a significant climax by my own pupil Richard A. Edwards in his definitive study *The Theology of Q*.[9] Bultmann simply did not have the resources to write a chapter like the chapter 4 of my *Introduction*, hence his understanding of the earliest Christian kerygma was necessarily inexact.[10] He necessarily could not see that early Christian apocalyptic drew its theological model from Jewish apocalyptic, as Jesus himself had not done, and that it interpreted Jesus, now, of course, understood as Jesus Christ, in terms of his function within this model. In other words, and this is the heart of my essay, early Christian apocalyptic developed a theological system based on a model that was not derived from Jesus, or from the Jesus tradition, and it interpreted Jesus and the Jesus tradition in light of the symbolic function of Jesus Christ within this overall theological system. So Jesus becomes not only Jesus Christ but also Jesus Son of Man, and as Jesus Son of Man his future coming is the anticipated eschatological event.[11] All this is, in my view, a far cry from anything Jesus himself taught, proclaimed, or implied.

Jesus Christ: The Unifying Factor

I have now reached the point of being able to indicate what I see as the unifying factor in the theology of the New Testament. That unifying factor in my view is the symbolic figure of Jesus, who is the constant in all the different theological systems developed in the New Testament. This symbolic figure is Jesus Christ, the faith or perspectival image rather than the historical Jesus, and he is constantly interpreted as functioning as the key element in theological systems not derived from the memory of the teaching of Jesus or from the ongoing Jesus tradition. But the fact remains that he is, as a symbolic figure, the one constant in the diversity of the New Testament.

Theological Systems in the New Testament

At this point I should obviously turn to a discussion of the theological systems developed by Hellenistic Jewish Mission Christianity, by Gentile Christianity, by Paul, and so on through the literature of emergent Catholicism and to a discussion of the symbolic function of the Jesus figure and the Jesus tradition in each and all of these theological systems. Nor will I make any secret of the fact that I think that such a discussion would provide a genuinely post-Bultmannian theology of the New Testament and that I have every intention of attempting it, although not here. I will restrict myself to a brief discussion drawing heavily on the material I presented in my *Introduction*. This procedure can be justified, I believe, both because of the limitations of space and also because the theology of the Synoptic Gospels and Acts is an area we have explored since Bultmann wrote and hence an area from which we may hope to derive genuinely post-Bultmannian insights.

Mark as Apocalyptic Drama

I turn then to the Gospel of Mark, which in my view is to be described as an apocalyptic drama. The Gospel of Mark narrates an apocalyptic "history" that began in the recent past with the "preaching" of John the Baptist and that continued with the Baptist being "delivered up" and the appearance of Jesus "preaching" and with Jesus being "delivered up." Then the Christians also "preach" and they are to be "delivered up," and the drama moves to its inevitable climax in the coming of Jesus as Son of Man. So the Gospel of Mark is a narrative drama in three acts. In act 1, John the Baptist appears, preaches, and is delivered up. In act 2, Jesus appears, preaches, and is delivered up. In act 3, the early Christians are depicted also as preaching and as being delivered up, and their being delivered up is a sign that the climactic coming of Jesus as Son of Man is imminent.

I want to stress the fact that it is my opinion that the commonly held view that the Gospel of Mark is "a passion narrative with an extended introduction" is only partially true. What dominates the Gospel of Mark is not so much the passion as the parousia of Jesus. The thrust of the Gospel is consistently *through* the passion *toward* the parousia. What the reader is left anticipating in 16:8 is not a resurrection appearance but the parousia in "Galilee." The climax that the Gospel of Mark anticipates is the coming of Jesus as Son of Man. The evangelist is concerned with a three-act apocalyptic drama that reaches its climax in that coming, a drama of which the story of Jesus is the second act.

Theologically speaking, the Gospel of Mark is rooted in Jewish apocalyptic. Daniel 7 is concerned with an apocalyptic drama in four acts (the four beasts/kingdoms) that reaches its climax in the coming of a "Son of Man," and that the evangelist Mark is thoroughly at home in Daniel 7 is obvious. What is new about the Gospel of Mark, theologically speaking, is not that the author saw himself and his readers as caught up in the final act of the apocalyptic drama—every apocalyptist thought in those terms—but that he sees the story of Jesus as the second act of that drama. It is the place given to the story of Jesus that breaks the apocalyptic mold. The story of Jesus *functions* for the evangelist as the second act of his three-act apocalyptic drama, but in its extent and significance it overpowers the other two acts, which is why Mark, who in many respects is an apocalyptist, ultimately becomes an evangelist, the author of a gospel rather than of an apocalypse.

The evangelist Mark sets out to narrate the preaching and the being delivered up of John the Baptist, of Jesus, and of the early Christians as the divinely ordained prelude to the coming of the apocalyptic redemption. Theologically speaking, this is, as I have claimed, the world of Jewish apocalyptic. But there is a new element in this drama, as compared with other such Jewish apocalyptic dramas, and that is that the Son of Man whose appearance will mark its climax is identical with the Jesus whose preaching and being delivered up constitute its second act. Because of this the teaching and example of Jesus take on a special significance. The Jesus whose coming as Son of Man will constitute the climax of the apocalyptic drama has already shown, by teaching and by example, how men and women should prepare themselves for that climax.

Now the idea of teaching in preparation for the coming redemption is a commonplace of Jewish apocalyptic. Every apocalyptic writer instructs and exhorts his readers to prepare themselves for the *eschaton* and even to facilitate its coming by acts of obedience, faithfulness, and endurance. In this respect the constant exhortations of the apocalyptist/evangelist Mark to correct belief (especially about Christology) and behavior (discipleship) are a commonplace of apocalyptic. What is new about them is the fact that it is the apocalyptic redeemer himself who gives the instruction and understanding necessary to the believer in preparation for the coming of Jesus as apocalyptic redeemer. Clearly there are major developments here from the more primitive theological world of early Christian apocalyptic, but the pattern of the symbolic figure of Jesus functioning within a theological system ultimately derived from Jewish apocalyptic remains the same.

Matthew and Luke-Acts as Foundation Myths

The Gospel of Matthew and the two-volume Luke-Acts are a generation later than the Gospel of Mark, but what is more important than the lapse of time itself is the fact that during that time there were dramatic changes in both the religious and the sociological situations of the early Christian communities. The Gospel of Mark was written under the circumstances of the Jewish War and with an imminent expectation of the parousia. The fall of Jerusalem and the destruction of the temple, if it has been experienced at all, is part of the final act of the apocalyptic drama. But Matthew and Luke are part of the generation that has had to learn to orient itself to the loss of the sacred center of the Judeo-Christian heritage, the Jerusalem temple. This is the change in the religious situation of the early Christian communities between Mark on the one hand, and Matthew and Luke-Acts on the other, and it would be difficult to exaggerate its importance. The sociological change is the fact that in this period the Christian communities become distinct sociological entities, finally separated from Judaism and hence confronted by the necessity to provide themselves with a theoretical base, a distinctive Christian foundation myth. This is also a change, the importance of which it would be difficult to exaggerate. In my view, both Matthew and Luke-Acts are to be interpreted in the context of an attempt to meet these two great needs of the middle period of New Testament Christianity: they successfully come to terms with the fall of Jerusalem, and they provide the Christian communities with a foundation myth of Christian origins. Moreover, as they do this they make significant use of the story of Jesus.

I cannot here repeat the detailed discussion of the Gospel of Matthew that I have given in my *Introduction,* but I will repeat the conclusion of that discussion since it summarizes my understanding of the Gospel.

> The fundamental changes in the gospel of Matthew compared to Mark are the birth stories at the beginning and the resurrection appearance and commissioning scene at the end. Mark himself gives only enough of an introduction to locate the story and identify the characters before he plunges into the first act of his three-act apocalyptic drama. But

Matthew does not think in terms of three-act apocalyptic drama, but rather of the time of Jesus as a special sacred time. By adding a genealogy and a series of stories on the birth and infancy of Jesus, by emphasizing Jesus as the new revelation fulfilling the promise of the old and superseding it, he is able to set the time of Jesus off from all previous time as the time of fulfillment.

The time of Jesus is then a special kind of time—of fulfillment, of revelation—and Matthew makes this point over and over in various ways. He uses the formula quotations to claim the time of Jesus as the time of fulfillment. He organizes the teaching of Jesus into five discourses, each ending with a formula, and the first taking place on a mountain, to claim that the teaching of Jesus is the new verbal revelation, the new Torah. Though he abbreviates miracle stories, he consistently heightens the sense of the miraculous, having two or many healed where in his source only one was healed, to stress the awesome nature of Jesus and his ministry.

But Matthew not only separates the time of Jesus from all previous time, he also separates it from all following time. Whereas Mark had deliberately involved his readers in the story and left them at the empty tomb awaiting the parousia in fear and trembling, Matthew just as deliberately separates his readers from the story by the Great Commission, in which Jesus appears as the risen and exalted Lord. The Great Commission envisages a time before the parousia, which will be of a different order from the time of Jesus. The revelation has now been given, and the need is for interpretation of that revelation and obedience to it. Now the disciples are to go out into all the world and make disciples; now, for the first time, the disciples are to teach, to interpret the revelation. Moreover, they are to organize into a church with a distinctive rite and formula of initiation: baptism in the name of the Trinity. Finally, the disciples will constantly be helped and their teaching authenticated by the presence of the risen Lord in their midst.[12]

In the Gospel of Matthew the story of Jesus becomes the basis for a foundation myth of Christian origins.

In my understanding of Luke-Acts I have been deeply influenced by Hans Conzelmann and his brilliant insight with regard to the Lukan *Heilsgeschichte* ["salvation history"].[13] In my *Introduction* I develop that insight, and I seek to ground it in a careful literary analysis of the two-volume work. In particular I regard the baptism/descent of the Spirit on Jesus as marking the beginning of *Die Mitte der Zeit* [lit. "the middle of time"], which I tend to represent in English as "the axis of salvation history," and the parallel baptism/descent of the

Spirit on the Church as the beginning of the third epoch of salvation history. I will restate the conclusions I reach in my *Introduction* with regard to Luke-Acts; they are as follows.

> The major difference between Mark and Luke-Acts is, of course, the sheer existence of the Acts of the Apostles itself. Mark could not possibly have written any such volume since he was anticipating an imminent parousia and envisaging his readers as preparing themselves for that event. The author of Luke-Acts, however, sees the parousia as deferred to the indefinite future and his readers as necessarily settling down to a long period of witnessing in the world. Under these circumstances an Acts of Apostles becomes necessary to help its readers understand how they came to be in their present position and give them a paradigm they can follow. This is the twofold purpose of Acts: it helps the readers understand their place and function in the world and its history by explaining to them the origin and development of the movement of which they are a part, and it helps them fulfill their function by giving them a model. In the Acts of the Apostles the almost legendary heroes of the early days of the church are deliberately presented as models of Christian witness in the world. Historically speaking, there were all kinds of differences between Peter and Paul, but in Acts they speak with one voice, share the same concerns, preach the same gospel; and the voice, concerns and gospel are those of the church of Luke's own time. Or perhaps it would be more accurate to say they are the voice, concerns, and gospel as Luke hopes they will become in his own time.

Both the gospel of Mark and the Acts of the Apostles are didactic history, a history of the past told to instruct the reader in the present. But they go about their task differently. The evangelist Mark puts his message on the lips of the authoritative figure of Jesus, who is Christ, Son of God and Son of Man. The author of Luke-Acts presents his message through the heroes of the church, Peter and Paul, who become models to be imitated, paradigmatic figures whose example should be followed. But the use of model figures does not end with the presentation of Peter and Paul in the Acts; it is extended to the figure of Jesus in the gospel of Luke. A remarkable feature of the gospel of Luke is the way Jesus is presented as a model of Christian piety, and the way parallels are carefully drawn between the practice of Jesus in the gospel and that of the apostles in the Acts. These parallels are then extended by implication to the readers of Luke-Acts, and the readers find themselves at one with Peter, Paul, Stephen, *and Jesus* in the world. For this reason the author of Luke-Acts plays down the christological emphases of his source, the gospel of Mark, and also avoids any soteriological emphasis in connection with the cross. The Jesus of the gospel of Luke is the first Christian, living out of the power of the spirit of God in the world. He is not the Jewish Messiah whose death ransoms men from the power of sin over them.

It is interesting to compare the different and yet sometimes similar reinterpretations of the gospel of Mark by the evangelist Matthew and by the author of Luke-Acts. The similarity is that both carefully separate the time of Jesus from all preceding or succeeding times. Matthew does so by birth stories at the beginning and the scene at the end; Luke by the descent of the Spirit at the beginning and the ascension at the end. Moreover, the similarity continues in that both emphasize the special nature of the time of Jesus; for both the time of Jesus is the time of fulfillment. Matthew does this with his constant use of formula quotations; Luke with his insistence on the absence of Satan between the temptation of Jesus and the plot to betray him, and also with the various portrayals of the time of Jesus as the center of time, distinct both from the time of "the law and the prophets" before it and the time of the preaching of "repentance and the forgiveness of sins to all nations" after it. Here is a sense, therefore, in which both Matthew and Luke transform what is essentially the apocalypse of Mark into a foundation myth of Christian origins.

But if Matthew and Luke both transform the apocalypse of Mark into a foundation myth, they go very different ways in portraying how their readers may relate to this foundation myth. For Matthew, the means is an authoritative interpretation of the verbal revelation that occurred in the Sacred Time of Jesus. For Luke, the means is an imitation of the Jesus of the Sacred Time, because for him Jesus is quite simply the first Christian. Luke sees Jesus as the primary example to be imitated, as he sees the heroes of the Christian church as secondary examples to be imitated. For him, Christian faith means essentially the imitation of Jesus and following the example of those heroes of the early church who did successfully imitate him.[14]

In Luke-Acts the story of Jesus has become the axis of salvation history and the foundation myth of Christian origins.

CONCLUSION

I am now in a position to pull together the threads of my argument. As the essential presupposition of the New Testament and its theology there stands the historical Jesus. Today, thanks to almost two hundred years of "Life-of-

Jesus Research" (*Leben-Jesu-Forschung*), we know a good deal about this Jesus.[15] In particular, in my view, we are in a position to make a statement about his theology. In the terms that I am using here we may say that Jesus had a theological model; there is a theological system in terms of which he consistently expressed himself. In *Jesus and the Language of the Kingdom*, I argue at length that what we may call the theology of Jesus is rooted and grounded in the ancient myth of sacral kingship and in the particularly Jewish form of this myth in which it is interwoven with elements from the ancient Israelite amphictyonic myth of salvation history. Historically speaking, Jesus consistently used the symbolic language that evoked this myth, and he was consistently able to mediate to his hearers the existential reality of the experience of God as King.

This historical Jesus is the presupposition of the New Testament and its theology, not its direct concern. The direct concern of the theology of the New Testament is the faith or perspectival image of Jesus, an image in which at the beginning the element of historical reminiscence must have played a considerable part. But as time went on, and as New Testament Christianity became a distinctive form of religious faith, this faith or perspectival image of Jesus became Jesus Christ, the dynamic and revelatory amalgam of the Jesus who was with the Christ who is.

It is this Jesus Christ who plays the determinative role in the various theological systems developed among the early Christian communities in New Testament times. The first such system of which we have direct knowledge is that represented by early Christian apocalyptic. This is a theological system derived from the world of Jewish apocalyptic, and within it Jesus functions as apocalyptic redeemer, as Son of Man. Theologically speaking, the Christian community that this theology represents was an apocalyptic sect within ancient Judaism, a sect very close in its theology to that represented by the Qumran texts or, for that matter, to the group that produced the "Similitudes of Enoch" (*1 Enoch* 37–71).[16]

But there was one fundamental difference between this early Christian community and the Qumran sect or the group that produced the Similitudes of Enoch and that is that the Jesus who was to be known as Son of Man had already been known as Jesus of Nazareth. The theological consequences of this we can see in the Gospel of Mark, where the theological system is still being derived from the world of Jewish apocalyptic but where the Jesus figure is bursting the bounds set for him by that system. For the first time the overall *story* of Jesus, the story from John the Baptist to the empty tomb, is told as an integral part of a theological system, and that story becomes too important to be regarded as simply the second act of a three-act apocalyptic drama.

In the generation following the first circulation of the Gospel of Mark there are major theological developments and sociological changes in the Christian communities. At the theological level there are major developments in the significance being attached to the story of Jesus as it is told and retold in the connected form it assumes in the Gospel of Mark. At the sociological level the Christian communities are faced with the necessity of developing their self-identity as the break with their Jewish heritage becomes more and more definite. Under these circumstances the story of Jesus comes to function as the foundation myth of Christian origins, a role it had not played before. These changes are particularly reflected in the Gospel of Matthew and in the two-volume Gospel of Luke and Acts of the Apostles.

The evangelist Matthew takes up a new theological model from his Jewish heritage, the model of the covenant, the model of Torah giving and of Torah obedience. He interprets the story of Jesus as the new sacred time of revelation, the time of the giving of the new and fulfilled verbal revelation of God to his people. The author of Luke-Acts takes up another and different model from the Jewish heritage of early Christianity, the model of salvation history, and he interprets the story of Jesus as the axis of that salvation history. Both "Matthew" and "Luke" take up models from their Jewish heritage, and both understand the story of Jesus as functioning within the framework provided by those models. But the Jesus story has become so important to each of them that it dominates the framework in which it is set, so that the theological framework becomes simply a means of interpreting the significance of Jesus Christ. At this point the story of Jesus becomes the foundation myth of Christian origins and the heart of New Testament theology.

I have deliberately chosen to discuss early Christian apocalyptic and the Synoptic Gospels and Acts since these are the areas within the New Testament in which significant work has been done since Bultmann wrote his *Theology of the New Testament*. I am arguing that this work does provide us with a genuinely post–Bultmannian approach to the theology of the New Testament as we recognize the function of the Jesus figure, the Jesus material, the Jesus story, within the different theological systems represented by early Christian apocalyptic and by the Synoptic Gospels and Acts. I am convinced that we can take a similar approach to the theological systems represented by Paul, John, and the literature of emergent Catholicism, but a discussion of those and other aspects of the theology of the New Testament must await another occasion. I will close by restating my thesis: the theology of the New Testament may be discerned as we follow the function of the Jesus figure, the Jesus material, the Jesus story in the theological systems developed within the New Testament. It is in the constantly developing theological function of this figure, material, story that I would find the thread that binds together the theology of the New Testament.[17]

8

The Challenge
of New Testament Theology

This essay is an attempt to present to the theological community of the University of Chicago Divinity School the challenge of the current discussion in New Testament theology as I see it.[1] It is concerned with New Testament *theology* because it is the theological aspect of New Testament studies—rather than the more technical aspects—which challenges the theological community at large; and it is concerned with New Testament theology *as I see it* because I can only present a challenge to you that I personally have felt and feel.

The challenge of New Testament theology today is very largely the challenge of one man: Rudolf Bultmann. It is he who has raised the questions with which we are wrestling, and his answers to these questions are the starting points for debates that have begun in Germany and reverberated around the world. In particular he has raised the two central questions in New Testament theology, to a discussion of which New Testament theologians challenge their colleagues in other theological disciplines: the problem of the historical Jesus and the question of demythologizing. As the discussion has developed these have become related to one another as two different aspects of the same ultimate question, but for the sake of convenience we will approach them separately.

THE PROBLEM OF THE HISTORICAL JESUS

The starting point here is Martin Kähler's challenge to the liberal "Life-of-Jesus Research" (*Leben-Jesu-Forschung*) that flourished in Germany in the nineteenth century and in America in the first half of the twentieth century. The characteristics of this movement are too well known to need elaboration here: the conviction that a life of Jesus could and should be written on the basis of material recoverable from the Synoptic Gospels and freely supplemented by insights derived from other historical figures by analogy, a life of Jesus that usually turned out to be a portrait of the author or of the author's ideals; the claim that the historical Jesus was the concern of faith and not the dogmatic Christ of the Church and the Gospels, and so on. Kähler's challenge to this movement is to be found in his lecture "The So-called Historical Jesus and the Historic, Biblical Christ," first published in 1892.[2] It consists of three points.

1. The argument that there is a valid distinction between the historical Jesus and the Christ of the Gospels: it is the distinction between the historical Jesus and the historic Christ, i.e., between the Jesus of history and the risen Lord in his fulfillment and his significance for later generations.
2. The claim that the historic Christ is the only object of Christian faith and not, repeat not, the historical Jesus.
3. The recognition of the fact that the Gospels are not and cannot be sources for a life of Jesus. They do not contain the necessary material, e.g., they have no account of his personal development, and attempts to supply this material by analogy are inappropriate to the subject and catastrophic in their consequences. The Gospels are products of early Christian preaching, the purpose of which is to proclaim the historic biblical Christ, or as Kähler liked to put it, the risen Christ in his fulfillment.

The subsequent discussion in Germany was in large part determined by the catastrophe of the First World War and its aftermath, which changed everything on the German theological scene. It completely destroyed liberalism with its interest in the historical Jesus and left the ground clear for the renaissance of Reformation theology spearheaded by Karl Barth. When, therefore, Bultmann took up the question in the 1920s he was writing in a different world, a world in which the effective death of liberalism and its Life-of-Jesus Research was recognized, in which a concept of faith quite different from the assumptions of liberal theology was accepted, and a world in which form criticism and existentialism were new and growing influences.

Bultmann's position can be summarized by beginning with the three points he takes over from Kähler and develops further himself.[3]

The Historical Jesus and the Historic Christ

There is a distinction between the historical Jesus and the historic Christ; it is the distinction between the one who proclaimed the Kingdom of God as the imminently to be expected eschatological act of God and the one who is himself proclaimed as the eschatological act of God. This is Bultmann's famous distinction between the Proclaimer and the Proclaimed. It should be noted that it includes three elements, all of which are very important to Bultmann.

1. The distinction between the historical Jesus and the historic Christ, derived from Martin Kähler.
2. The introduction of a reference to the eschatological act of God, proclaimed by Jesus in terms of the Kingdom of God and by the early church in terms of the cross and resurrection of Christ. So far as the message of Jesus is concerned this comes from the "thoroughgoing eschatology" (*konsequente Eschatologie*) of Johannes Weiss and Albert Schweitzer that Bultmann has taken up and demythologized; so far as the message of the early Church is concerned it is Bultmann's own interpretation, largely derived from an exegesis of Paul and John.
3. The emphasis upon the fact that in the message of Jesus this eschatological act of God is still future, albeit imminent and even now beginning to break in, whereas in the kerygma of the early Church it is already past, although available ever anew as God manifests himself as eschatological event in the kerygma. So Bultmann always maintains that salvation is only a promise in the message of Jesus but a present reality through the kerygma of the Church. This again, so far as the message of Jesus is concerned, is derived from "consequent eschatology" and it has been furiously debated for the last half century, as I have shown elsewhere.[4]

The Object of Faith

The object of Christian faith is the historic Christ, the Christ of the kerygma and not the historical Jesus. This insight, derived from Kähler and developed by Bultmann, owes much to the revival of Reformation theology in Germany after the First World War to which I have already referred. It is also a point at which it becomes clear that Bultmann is both a Lutheran and an existentialist. As a Lutheran he sees the ultimate context of faith as the Word of God—that is for him the kerygma of the early Church; and he sees faith as necessarily independent of any factors external to this context. As an existentialist he sees the ultimate moment as a moment of decision in the context of confrontation. Put these things together and we have faith arising by decision as the individual is confronted by the Christ present in the kerygma. Everything else finds its place in reference to this central aspect of Bultmann's theology. This moment of faith is the consummation to which all else is subsidiary and upon which all else is dependent. Appropriately enough, the finest discussion of Bultmann's theology to be found in any language, by the German-speaking Roman Catholic Gotthold Hasenhüttl, is titled simply *Der Glaubensvollzug* (Faith: The Consummation).[5]

Faith arises by decision out of confrontation with the Christ of the kerygma, the Christ present in the kerygma. The presence of Christ in the kerygma is, for Bultmann, the meaning of the resurrection. He says that the resurrection is Christ risen in the kerygma and the Easter faith is faith in the Christ present in the kerygma. The presence of Christ in the kerygma is the eschatological act of God and confrontation with this Christ is the eschatological event.

The Christ present in the kerygma is necessarily distinct from the historical Jesus, above all in what we may call his effectiveness. The historical Jesus did not demand faith in himself but at the most in his word, especially in his word of proclamation of the imminence of the Kingdom of God. Moreover, he did not offer salvation but only promised it for the future. The kerygma, however, does demand faith in the Christ present in it and it offers salvation now to those who believe in him. Again, the historical Jesus proclaimed the future eschatological event, whereas the kerygmatic Christ is the eschatological event as he confronts the man addressed by the kerygma. The historical Jesus proclaimed a message that was the last word of God before the End; the kerygmatic Christ is the word of God and the End.

Lastly on this point, we come to the Reformation principle "by faith alone" as it was restated by Kähler, maintained by Bultmann and as it was generally acceptable in the Germany in which liberal theology was dead and Reformation theology in revival: faith as such is necessarily independent of historical facts, even historical facts about Jesus. In practice today's assured historical facts tend to become tomorrow's abandoned historians' hypotheses, and in principle a faith built upon historical fact would not be faith at all but a work. Further, faith is faith in the eschatological act of God in Jesus Christ, but that God has acted in Jesus Christ is not a fact of past history open to historical verification; this is shown by the way in which the New Testament describes the figure and work of Christ in mythological and not historical terms.

The Gospels

The Gospels are not and cannot be sources for a life of Jesus; they are products and embodiments of the preaching of the early Church. This third point of Kähler's is taken up and developed by Bultmann, to whom indeed it is very important. Form criticism reinforced Kähler's point by showing how very far and in what remarkable ways the Gospels are dependent upon the preaching and kerygma of the early Church. Bultmann is a leading form critic and he has shown convincingly that the gospel form was created to give literary form to the kerygma of the early Church and that the gospel material has been shaped by, and was to a large extent created for, the use made of it in the kerygma.[6]

As a theologian, Bultmann has taken seriously the consequences of his work as a New Testament critic. Indeed one of the most attractive things about his work is the ruthless honesty with which, as a theologian, he accepts the consequences of his work as a critical scholar. His critical studies convinced him that the Gospels as such are necessarily concerned with only one historical fact: the "thatness" of Jesus and his cross. That there was a Jesus and that he was crucified is the necessary historical presupposition for the kerygma. But beyond this the Synoptic Gospels themselves seem to be uninterested in the historical element as such, since they freely overlay the historical with the mythical. Much of the material they present is a historicization of myth, and they make absolutely no attempt to distinguish the historical as such from the mythical. They are a unique combination of historical report and kerygmatic Christology, the purpose of which is, however, through and through, proclamation and not historical reporting. This is even more clearly true of Paul and John, both of whom require no more than the "that" of the life of Jesus and his crucifixion for their proclamation. So the nature and purpose of the Gospels as this is revealed by critical scholarship support Bultmann's understanding of the significance of the historical Jesus for Christian faith.

Jesus and Existence

In addition to the three aspects developed from Kähler there is one further element in Bultmann's thinking that needs to be considered at this point: the significance of the historical Jesus for an individual's self-understanding, or understanding of existence.

Here let me pause to say that the term is self-understanding and not self-consciousness, a point that becomes significant in the post–Bultmannian debate. By self-understanding Bultmann means the understanding that the self comes to concerning the nature of its historical existence. In his *History and Eschatology,* originally written in English,[7] he often uses the phrase in close connection with the untranslatable German word *Weltanschauung,* and we are to understand it as referring to a person looking at the existence that is his or hers and reaching an understanding of it in all its historicity. The actual word in German is *Existenzverständnis.* James M. Robinson has properly urged that we use the English "understanding of existence" to express it.[8] The problem is to grasp that we mean by understanding of the self's own existence (what else is possible for an existentialist?), but at the same time we do not mean the subjective *self*-understanding where the emphasis is upon the self rather than the self's existence. The distinction might be expressed as a distinction between the self's understanding of its existence and the conscious decisions, deeds, and words to which this understanding leads and in which it may be expressed.

Bultmann espouses an existentialist understanding of historiography whereby the individual enters into dialogue with the past and is challenged by an understanding of existence (self-understanding) from the past that becomes significant to him in the historicity of his own existence. So, in the case of the historical Jesus, an understanding of existence (self-understanding, not self-consciousness) is revealed in his teaching that challenges us in terms of our understanding of our own existence. Hence Bultmann writes a Jesus book, *Jesus and the Word,* from this perspective.

Three things must, however, be said at this point.

1. As the subject of this existentialist historiography Jesus is not unique. A similar study, with similar consequences in terms of a possible challenge to our understanding of existence, could be carried out in connection with any figure from the past for whom we have sources: Socrates the philosopher, or even Attila the Hun, as well as Jesus the Christ.

2. This historiographical challenge to our self-understanding is not for Bultmann the challenge of faith, not even though the challenge of faith could be, and is, expressed by him in similar existentialistic terminology. He himself stresses that the Jesus of history is not kerygmatic and that his book *Jesus and the Word* is not kerygma,[9] because the essential aspect of the kerygma is that Christ is present in it as eschatological event, and Christ is not so present in existentialist historiographical studies of the historical Jesus. If he were then they would cease to be existentialist historiographical studies and become kerygma.

3. This type of study of Jesus is to be sharply distinguished from the liberal Quest. In the liberal Quest attempts were made to reach and to understand the psychology and personality of Jesus (that is, his self-consciousness)—an endeavor that was both impossible (no sources) and illegitimate (use of analogy)—whereas in the Bultmann study the concern is with the understanding of existence (self-understanding) revealed in the teaching of Jesus.

Critiques

This position of Bultmann's on the question of the historical Jesus and his significance for faith has been attacked from three standpoints. One might say from the right, left, and center.

From the Right

The attack from the right has turned on the conviction that the historical nature of the Christian faith, or the meaning of the Incarnation, necessitates more emphasis upon the actual historical events *circa* 30 C.E. than Bultmann will allow. In this camp we find all kinds of strange comrades in arms united in their conviction that the historical events of the ministry of Jesus, in addition to the cross, are necessary to the Christian faith. We can find the whole gamut of possibilities ranging from the extreme conservative, who insists on the factual historicity of everything from the Virgin Birth to the Resurrection, to the old-fashioned liberal for whom only the Jesus reconstructed by historical study can be of significance to faith.

Of all the possible names here I will mention only that of my own teacher, the moderately conservative Joachim Jeremias, who deserves to be heard on this point because he has done more than any other single scholar to add to our knowledge of the historical Jesus. He has published a booklet on the question that I have translated.[10] In this he argues that the proclamation is not itself revelation, but it leads to revelation. Thus the historical Jesus is the necessary and only presupposition of the kerygma (a play on Bultmann's famous opening sentence of his *Theology of the New Testament*), since only the Son of Man and his word, by which Jeremias means the historical Jesus and his teaching, can give authority to the proclamation. This is a major issue in the contemporary debate: Does Bultmann's view do less than justice to the historical nature of the Christian faith? Does it do violence to the Incarnation? Is the historical Jesus as such the necessary ultimate concern to whom the kerygma points?

From the Left
The attack from the left has taken the opposite position, namely that Bultmann is inconsistent in his views in that he properly sees Christian faith as a transition from inauthentic to authentic existence (more on this under "Demythologizing" below) and then illogically maintains a necessary link with the historical Jesus in this process. Surely he should recognize the fact that all he is really saying is that there are those for whom this is true. But there are those for whom the transition can be made in other ways.

There is, in particular, the existentialist philosopher Karl Jaspers who debated this issue with Bultmann,[11] maintaining that the link with the historical Jesus introduces an objective factor into an existential moment where it has no place. Jaspers's views are actually in one respect reminiscent of liberalism of the Harnack variety in that he sees Jesus as an example—an example of the kind of existential relationship to the transcendent that the philosopher seeks for himself. It must be admitted that Jaspers appears to have the better of his immediate argument with Bultmann, Bultmann's final reply having been a three-sentence letter refusing to commit himself further at that time. But he returned to the discussion later, in a quite different context, and then it became obvious that he regarded himself as committed by the New Testament itself to a necessary link with the historical Jesus. For he could only reiterate his major point, that the Christian faith as such is committed to the paradoxical assertion that a historical event within time, Jesus and his cross, is the eschatological event, and then support it by exegesis of New Testament texts, especially Paul and John.

Thus we come to the unbridgeable gap between the New Testament theologian and the theistic existentialist, and we find that it is an old issue returning in a new form: Is the historical Jesus necessarily anything more than an example that we seek to imitate in his worship of the Father (Harnack) or in his breakthrough to true existential self-understanding (Jaspers)?

From the Center

The attack from the center is not really an attack at all but a re-raising of the question of the historical Jesus from within the circle of Bultmann's own pupils. It is convenient but somewhat misleading to speak of the "new quest of the historical Jesus" insofar as this implies a homogeneous group moving in a definite direction.[12] The only elements of homogeneity in this group are the fact that they all began by accepting Bultmann's general position and that they all nonetheless agreed that he had not settled the question of the historical Jesus. From that point they take off on their own and any two or three of them in agreement today will almost certainly not be in agreement tomorrow. Also Bultmann's position turns out to be stronger than it first appears; a number of "new questers" have ended up back in the fold with the master, and more will probably do so.

The most important member of this group is, in my view, still the man who first raised the question: Ernst Käsemann, whose 1953 essay is now available in English.[13] Three points from this essay have proven to be of real significance. In the first place, Käsemann sounded a warning about the danger of a position in which there was no real and material continuity between the historical Jesus and the kerygmatic Christ: the danger of falling into docetism or of having faith degenerate into a mere mysticism or moralism. This kind of thing had, of course, been said often enough by opponents of Bultmann from the right; but now it was being said by a member of the "Bultmann school"—a fact that gave it great weight.

Even so, in itself, such a warning might not have been regarded as too significant—except by Bultmann's opponents!—had it not been for the fact that Käsemann supported it by observing that the Synoptic Gospel tradition is in fact more concerned with the historical Jesus than Bultmann had allowed. This was really important because Bultmann's strength had always been that his position is supported by his understanding and exegesis of the New Testament. But his exegesis is really determined by what he learns from Paul and

John. Käsemann raised the question of the Synoptic tradition, pointing out that the Synoptic tradition is not uniform in its own understanding of the relationship between past fact and present faith. The Gospels are in agreement that the "once" of Jesus' life history has become the "once for all" of revelation, the *chronos* of Jesus having become the *kairos* of faith. But the relationship between the now of the kerygma and the then of the historical Jesus is a problem for which they find no solution; or rather it is a problem for which they find their several different solutions. So Käsemann is able to claim that the problem of the historical Jesus is a problem that the New Testament itself bequeaths to us, and the complexity of the New Testament tradition on this point must warn us that it is by no means easy to do justice to both the "now" and the "then."

Thirdly, Käsemann investigated our actual knowledge of the historical Jesus and showed convincingly that we know enough about his teaching to be able to say that the messiahship explicit in the kerygma is already implicit in the teaching of Jesus. Thus we stumble across a real element of continuity; for all the discontinuity between the historical Jesus and the kerygmatic Christ, there is real continuity between the preaching of Jesus and the preaching about him. This seemed to Käsemann to offer real hope as a line of approach to the problem bequeathed to us by the New Testament and not satisfactorily solved by Bultmann.

At this point Käsemann's article ends, and it is easy to see why it created the furor that it did. It raises questions and suggests lines of approach without really offering any solution of its own. Certainly it marked the beginning of all kinds of intensive work and interesting developments. The question of the historical Jesus had been raised in its modern form.

Every suggestion that Käsemann made has been intensively followed up. The theology of the Synoptic tradition, and of the differing strata in that tradition, has become a major field for investigation. Some of the work done here can only be called brilliant.[14] The question of the parallels between the message of Jesus and the message about him has been explored from every conceivable angle, even from the perspective of Qumran—the Dead Sea Scrolls had to be brought into the act somehow![15]

It is in this exploration of the parallels between the message of Jesus and the message about him that the most characteristic work of the "post-Bultmannians" has been done. They have attempted, and are attempting, to explore the relevance of the historical Jesus for the Christian faith from this point of departure. Probably the best-known examples here are the work of James M. Robinson,[16] and Ernst Fuchs[17] and Gerhard Ebeling on the other.[18] Robinson accepted the parallels pointed out by Käsemann, Günther Bornkamm, and others and added to them some of his own derived from a study of the Kingdom of God sayings. Then, in addition, he took the existentialist modern historiography that seeks to mediate an encounter with the past at the level of self-understanding and approached the historical Jesus and his message in this way. Now, you see, we have two sets of parallels: between the historical Jesus and the kerygmatic Christ at the level of meaning of the message of and about the one and the other, and the encounters mediated by modern historiography with the one and kerygmatic proclamation with the other. The encounter with the historical Jesus then becomes significant for faith, not because it replaces or makes unnecessary the encounter with the kerygmatic Christ, but because it serves to correct, supplement, and give content to the faith that arises here and only here.

May I say in passing that although I would want to express the matter in a somewhat different, and perhaps less ambitious, manner this seems to me to be a most valid and promising approach to the question.

Fuchs and Ebeling are the post-Bultmannians who have traveled farthest along the road of the "New Quest." Indeed they have gone so far that they are no longer to be contained in these categories and must now be reckoned as having achieved a new and distinctive theological position, a position that is generally designated the "New Hermeneutic."[19] We will consider them together since the differences between them are insignificant in the immediate context of our discussion.

They begin by exploring the concept of "faith as the parallel between the historical Jesus and the kerygmatic Christ." They argue that Jesus himself reached a decision in the context of a confrontation with God in which he decides for the love and forgiveness of God and accepts the consequences of suffering (Fuchs) and by reason of which he may properly be designated the witness of faith (Ebeling). Indeed it may be said that faith is manifested in Jesus or, as they put it, faith comes to word or becomes a word-event in him (Ebeling), faith comes to language or becomes a language-event in him (Fuchs). Similarly, faith becomes a word- or language-event for the believer in the kerygma as the believer echoes the decision first made by Jesus (Fuchs). Since faith is the constant, the purpose of exegesis is to find a way in which faith may come to word or language in the New Testament texts for the believer.

I appreciate the fact that this bald summary is only a caricature of this most recent development; but I hope it is sufficient to show that we do indeed have here a new theological position. By pushing the Lutheran emphasis upon faith to an extreme Fuchs and Ebeling have arrived at a point at which faith is practically personified. By taking the Lutheran emphasis upon the Word to a similar extreme they have achieved a concept of faith coming into being or being manifested in "word" or "language," and so have made a new use of the parallel between the message of Jesus and the message about Jesus. By being prepared to think of decisions that Jesus himself made and in which the believer imitates him, they have reached a point at which they are restating a position that Schleiermacher and Harnack would surely have recognized despite the difference in conceptualization.

Bultmann has reacted very sharply against this development that he accuses of psychologizing about Jesus in the manner of an already discredited liberalism.[20] In light of Bultmann's criticism Ebeling carefully restated his position,[21] making the following points:

1. It is not a case of psychologizing about Jesus but of recognizing that a person is necessarily involved in his or her word, that the message necessarily involves the messenger, that a message challenging to faith necessarily involves a witnessing to faith on the part of the messenger.
2. Bultmann himself speaks of the Proclaimer becoming the Proclaimed. In the new terminology Ebeling is using, this is expressed as the witness to faith becoming the ground of faith.
3. The kerygma as such is kerygma by act of God, but it needs historical knowledge for its proper interpretation. Since it identifies kerygmatic Christ and historical Jesus, knowledge of the historical Jesus may properly be used to interpret the kerygma.

It is clear that we are only at the beginning of what promises to be a most lively discussion. I will say something more about the New Hermeneutic in the next section.

THE QUESTION OF DEMYTHOLOGIZING

The question of the historical Jesus and the question of demythologizing are ultimately two different aspects of the same question.[22] Since I have discussed the first in such detail as is possible in one paper, I can be briefer in connection with the second. Demythologizing is an attempt to break through to what is essential in the New Testament message and then to find a way of expressing it that will be meaningful to modern people. It is based upon two assumptions: (1) that the message of the New Testament is expressed in terms that are meaningless to mid-twentieth-century theological people; and (2) that nonetheless, the New Testament message is descriptive of a reality that is meaningful to those people, indeed essential to his or her true being as a human.

The New Testament is expressed in terms of a three-story view of the universe, of a world dominated by spirits good and evil: in other words, in terms of myth.[23] Further, the New Testament speaks of what it considers the ultimate realities of life equally in terms of myth: death as a punishment for sin, guilt as expiated by the death of a sinless man, a resurrection that releases a living supernatural power through the sacraments, and so on. But modern people do not think in these terms and therefore the message becomes meaningless to them. This is a false stumbling block (*skandalon*); offended by the terms in which it is expressed, modern people do not come face-to-face with the challenge of the message itself. Or, the other possibility, they sacrifice their intellects and understanding in order to accept the mythology and so come to a false kind of faith, and they come to it as less than whole persons.

Facing this challenge, Bultmann sought to express the reality of the Christian gospel in terms of a modern existentialist understanding of being human. He argued that humans are indeed fallen in that as humans they have a possibility of authentic existence that in fact they do not achieve. What for them is a possibility in principle is not a possibility in fact. The one thing that can transform the possibility in principle to a possibility in fact is the act of God. True existence, the full realization of human possibilities as humans, is only available in faith; existence in faith is the only authentic existence.

The act of God that makes faith a possibility is the eschatological act of God in the kerygma of the Church. For Bultmann, this is a combination of the historical cross of Jesus and the mythical resurrection; but as proclaimed by the Church it becomes truly historic as God addresses humanity through it with the offer and challenge of authentic existence.

Three things about Bultmann's theology need to be stressed at this point.[24]

1. For Bultmann, the believer and the object of belief belong inextricably together. Revelation and faith, word and hearing, encounter and understanding belong together and must be held together because they live only in their relationship to one another. There can be no meaning for one without the other. Consequently, we can never speak of God without at the same time speaking of humanity. Revelation of God has to be consummated in encounter with humanity; without this it is not truly revelation. So whenever we speak of revelation or salvation event we must at the same time be speaking of humans who are called to hear and to believe.

2. There is in Bultmann's proposal for demythologizing a deliberate existentializing and personalizing of eschatology. The eschaton is God's freeing word addressed to man in the proclamation of the Church. This proclamation is the proclamation of the cross and resurrection as the eschatological act of God, and this eschatological act is realized for me as I find myself addressed by God through the proclamation of the Church. It is, so to speak, personalized for me as it becomes God's eschatological act for me in my eschatological moment.

3. The key to understanding Bultmann's position is perhaps the idea of paradoxical identity. There is a paradoxical identity of proclamation and saving event as the saving event becomes the saving event for me in the proclamation. There is the paradoxical identity, above all, of eschatology and history in the cross that is at one and the same time eschatological and historical event. This is the absolutely necessary paradox, the one essential historical aspect of the eschatological event being the "thatness" of Christ and his cross.

Critiques

As with the question of the historical Jesus, there is a right, left, and center reaction to Bultmann's demythologizing proposal; and the same people tend to be arrayed on the same sides in the discussion of the two questions.

From the Right

On the right there are many theologians who claim that Bultmann has done less than justice to the objective element in the salvation process, that in his anxiety to speak meaningfully to humanity he has ceased to speak meaningfully of God. The best-known name here is that of Karl Barth,[25] who argues that Bultmann has not done justice to the Christ-event as significant in itself apart altogether from humanity's appropriation of that significance. He has failed to do justice to the fact that Christ was crucified and resurrected in the past and that faith is the appropriation of the benefits of that past historical event. For Bultmann it is as though the crucifixion and resurrection first take place in the attitude and experience of the believer. In his attempt to avoid a one-sided objectivism, Bultmann has fallen into an equally one-sided subjectivism.

From the Left

Of the critics from the left, the best-known names are probably Karl Jaspers in Europe[26] and Schubert Ogden in America.[27] These claim that Bultmann is wrong in seeing in the Christ-event the only possibility for authentic existence. Here he is inconsistent, they claim, in that, having properly rid himself of mythology and having properly interpreted reality existentially, he has illogically retained one element of myth: the cross and resurrection of Jesus as eschatological act of God and as essential to authentic existence. If the possibility of authentic existence is a possibility offered to humanity by God, and Jaspers and Ogden would both agree that it is, then it must be seen as offered in many ways and not only through the one event. As we have already seen, Jaspers would view Jesus as an example to be imitated. Ogden, on the other hand, claims that the unconditioned gift and demand of God's love is the ground of humanity's possibility of authentic existence and that this is decisively manifested in Jesus. It is decisively manifested in Jesus, but we may not say that it is manifested nowhere else. We must recognize that it is addressed to people in every aspect and event of their lives. Where Jaspers sees Jesus as the example of authentic existence to be imitated, Ogden sees the event of encounter with Jesus as only one possible way of encountering the gift and demand of God's love wherein lies the possibility of authentic existence, even if it is the most important way.

From the Center

Unfortunately, I have no time to discuss possible replies to these reactions from the right and the left but must turn immediately to the center, where we have many developments with again the most far-reaching being the New Hermeneutic of Fuchs and Ebeling.[28] They pick up the emphasis upon demythologizing as an existentialist interpretation of the New Testament, but they come to it in light of their emphasis upon faith's concern with the historical Jesus and not exclusively with the kerygma, as is the case with Bultmann. For them, as we noted earlier, faith comes to word or language in Jesus for those who heard his message and for subsequent generations in the Church's message about him. This is the continuity of proclamation and the continuity of faith coming to word or language in proclamation for the believer. So far as we are concerned the primary source in which we hear the word being proclaimed is the New Testament. Thus the New Testament is to be interpreted in such a manner as to facilitate the coming of faith to word or language for us through its words. A true existentialist interpretation of the New Testament is one through which faith comes to be word- or language-event for us; and the hermeneutic by means of which this is to be achieved is the New Hermeneutic.

Here we have a new and interesting development in which hermeneutic has in effect taken the place of kerygma, and in which a concern for an existentialist interpretation of the kerygma has been modified by a concern for the historical Jesus until it has become a concern for an existentialist interpretation of the New Testament—now seen not as a sourcebook for knowledge of the historical Jesus, as in the older liberalism, but as a means whereby that faith that came to word or language in Jesus may come to be word- or language-event for us. James M. Robinson appropriately suggests that this position be designated "neo-liberalism."

The New Hermeneutic is an appropriate place at which to call a halt to this all too brief and cursory review of some of the challenging issues of contemporary New Testament theology. For in a sense we have come full circle, from nineteenth-century liberalism to the twentieth-century neo-liberalisms of the New Hermeneutic.

CONCLUSION

In a brief conclusion, may I point to some of the issues raised by these developments in New Testament theology and challenging all theologians to discussion? I am deliberately omitting the detailed issues that concern only the New Testament as such.

In the first place, we have the challenges that can be summed up under the rubric "Faith and History." What is the nature of faith and its relation to history, of history and its relation to faith? There can be no doubt that these are vital questions. It is very important that they should be taken up by theology as a whole, and that they should be taken up by theologians who are equipped to discuss them with emphases other than the Lutheran approach to faith and the existentialist approach to history that tend to be dominant among contemporary New Testament theologians. Personally I am inclined to think that these particular emphases will turn out to be dominant after all, not because of the historical accident that the leading New Testament theologians today tend to be Lutherans and existentialists, but because they will prove to be the categories most appropriate to the problems—and I say this as a liberal Baptist, but perhaps the discussion will prove me wrong!

Secondly, we have the problems that can be included in the category "Humanity and God," if you will forgive the obvious naiveté of such a rubric. How should a person think of himself or herself and his or her existence? How can a person think of God? How may one think of Christ in relation to human existence on the one hand and God on the other? These are, of course, perennial theological problems; but they surely have new force and vigor as a consequence of the intensive discussion going on in New Testament theology and the variety of positions there represented. It is in connection with this group of questions that I believe the American theological situation will prove to have a particular contribution to make, for in American theology we have a much more radical skepticism about what my colleague Langdon Gilkey calls "the possibility of God-language" than is the case in the predominantly German-oriented New Testament theology.[29] And we also have over here a concern for the realities of human existence that demand expression in categories other than the existentialist. Both of these factors need to find expression in the discussion.

Lastly, we have the group of questions that may be summed up under the heading "The Word of God." We have seen how New Testament theology has been exploring the manifold issues raised here: the word of God as medium of revelation or the context of the salvation-event; the kerygma of the Church as the word of God; the word of Jesus and the word about Jesus; and, most recently, faith as word- or language-event and the hermeneutical task as the central theological task. It is, I think, clear that one thing urgently needed is further discussion of these issues, perhaps particularly those raised by the New Hermeneutic, on the basis of an ontology and epistemology other than the existentialist. An assault on the New Hermeneutic from the standpoint of a linguistic analytical philosophy would be a real contribution to our discussion. Another thing urgently needed at this point is a discussion of New Testament hermeneutics in general from the standpoint of the findings of general literary criticism. It is, after all, not only in the field of New Testament studies that we face the problem of myth and the question of a present understanding of a text from the distant past. General literary critics have been wrestling with these problems every bit as intensively as have Bultmann and his followers, and it is high time that their findings came to word in our discussion. This is perhaps particularly a task for the English language discussion for the simple reason that literary criticism flourishes much more strongly today in Britain and America than it does in Germany. Here in Chicago we might feel a particular responsibility for this aspect of the discussion since we have an emphasis upon theology and literature in our divinity school and a number of most eminent literary critics working and teaching in the humanities division of the university.

Notes

N.B.: Notes added by the editor are indicated by the number in square brackets [1.]. If added to the end of an original note, this is indicated by [Ed.] preceding the editor's addition.

1. THE KINGDOM OF GOD—
INTERPRETING A BIBLICAL SYMBOL

1. I am particularly sensitive to the fact that I do not discuss any Jewish interpretation of the symbol after New Testament times; but in the space of one article it seemed best to stay within one tradition, the Christian. [Ed.] See now Dennis C. Duling, "The Kingdom of God, Kingdom of Heaven: OT, Early Judaism, and Hellenistic Usage," in *ABD* 4.49–56.

2. Sigmund Mowinckel, *The Psalms in Israel's Worship*, trans. D. R. Ap-Thomas (Nashville: Abingdon, 1962) 1.114.

[3.] For each of these deities, see the articles in *Dictionary of Deities and Demons in the Bible*, ed. Karel van der Toorn, Bob Becking, and Pieter W. van der Horst, 2nd ed. (Leiden: Brill, 1999): Tzvi Abusch, "Marduk," 543–49; Alasdair Livingstone, "Assur," 108–9; Emile Puech, "Milcom," 575–76; Sergio Ribichini, "Melqart," 563–65; and Karel van der Toorn, "Yahweh," 910–19.

4. Mowinckel, *Psalms*, 1.107. The English translations all have "The LORD reigns" or the equivalent. RSV: "The LORD reigns"; NEB: "The LORD is king"; JB: "Yahweh is king."

5. Mowinckel, *Psalms*, 1.125: "the concept of Yahweh as a king would hardly be adopted by the Israelites until they themselves had got a king, and, with him, an obvious occasion to bestow on Yahweh the highest title of honor."

6. Gerhard von Rad, "The Problem of the Hexateuch," in *The Problem of the Hexateuch and Other Essays*, trans. E. W. T. Dicken (New York: McGraw-Hill, 1966) 1–78. This insight is developed further in von Rad's *Old Testament Theology*, vol. 1: *The Theology of Israel's Historical Traditions*, trans. D. M. G. Stalker (New York: Harper & Row, 1962).

[7.] For a systematic treatment of these traditions, see Martin Noth, *A History of Pentateuchal Traditions*, trans. B. W. Anderson (Englewood Cliffs, N.J.: Prentice Hall, 1972).

8. In the monarchial period the salvation history was extended to include the foundation of the monarchy and the united kingdom and the establishment of

the temple at Jerusalem. It was also expanded to include the theophany and giving of the Law at Sinai, an element conspicuously absent from the early formulations to which von Rad called attention. The relationship between the Sinai tradition and the other elements of the salvation history is a matter of dispute among the competent scholars. For recent discussions, see Frank Moore Cross, *Canaanite Myth and Hebrew Epic: Essays in the History of the Religion of Israel* (Cambridge: Harvard Univ. Press, 1973) 79–90; and E. W. Nicholson, *Exodus and Sinai in History and Tradition*, GPT (Atlanta: John Knox, 1974).

9. Mowinckel, *Psalms*, 1.108.

[10.] This rendering omits the liturgical refrain in the MT that concludes each line: "for his steadfast love endures for ever."

11. The original narrative of the creation plus salvation history must have included an account of the conquest of Canaan; that is, the account must have gone from Numbers to Joshua. "The break which the Book of Deuteronomy causes between the narratives in the Book of Numbers and those in Joshua is unnatural in the extreme," James A. Sanders, *Torah and Canon* (Philadelphia: Fortress Press, 1972) 25.

12. From the point of view of linguistic usage, the form "Kingdom of God" is comparatively late; it may even be specifically Christian. Ancient Judaism tended to use "Kingdom" with a personal pronoun referring to God ("his," "your"), or to use the verb with God as subject. In the New Testament era, the Jews were using the form "Kingdom of Heaven," where Heaven was a circumlocution for God. It should be recognized that there is no satisfactory English translation of the Hebrew or Aramaic phrases involved. I constantly use "Reign or Kingdom" to indicate the dynamic force of the original noun; and where I use "Kingdom" alone, "Reign or" is to be understood as implied.

[13.] In his original article, Perrin referred to Exodus 15 as "the song of Moses." Even though he does not capitalize "song"—thus using it in a mere descriptive sense—for clarity I have changed this to "Song of the Sea," its more common designation among scholars. "The Song of Moses" is usually used for Deut 32:1-43.

[14.] For a perceptive analysis of various viewpoints regarding Exodus 15, see Stan Rummel, "Narrative Structures in the Ugaritic Texts," in *Ras Shamra Parallels*, vol. 3 (Rome: Pontifical Biblical Institute Press, 1981) 236–60 [221–332].

15. Philip Wheelwright, *Metaphor and Reality* (Bloomington: Indiana Univ. Press, 1962) 239. A problem in this particular discussion is that we are dealing with different kinds of myth. On the one hand, we have the myth of creation, the cosmogonic myth, mediated to Israel by its Canaanite neighbors and forming the basis for the slightly different myth of the Kingship of God. Then, on the other hand, we have the salvation history myth, the myth of God active as King in the history of the Israelite people. Because of the link with history in the case of the salvation history myth, some scholars tend to resist the use of the word "myth" in this connection. Cross, for example, prefers to speak of "epic," and the title of his book, *Canaanite Myth and Hebrew Epic*, expresses his understanding of the contrast between the cosmogonic myth and the epic of the redemptive history (Cross prefers history-of-redemption to salvation history to represent the German *Heilsgeschichte;* see Cross, 83). But the element of

history involved in the *Heilsgeschichte* does not make it any less a myth in the sense of Watts's definition, which I accept as a valid definition of this kind of myth. The cosmogonic myth and the salvation history myth are different kinds of myths, but they are both myths, and they both function as myths in ancient Israel, especially as they are amalgamated. Moreover, the salvation history myth continues to function as myth right into the present, as we shall argue in the course of this essay. For an introductory discussion of the element of history in biblical myths see Perrin, *The New Testament: An Introduction* (New York: Harcourt Brace Jovanovich, 1974) 21–33.

[16.] Amos Niven Wilder, longtime professor of New Testament at Harvard University, was with the American Ambulance Field Service during World War I. He recounted his experiences in *Armageddon Revisited: A World War I Journal* (New Haven: Yale Univ. Press, 1994).

[17.] Albert Schweitzer, *The Quest of the Historical Jesus*, 1st complete ed., trans. S. M. Cupitt, ed. John Bowden, FCBS (Minneapolis: Fortress Press, 2000).

18. The investigation of Jesus' proclamation of the Kingdom of God, and the question of its proper interpretation, has concerned me all my academic life. My publications on the subject, in chronological order, are as follows: *The Kingdom of God in the Teaching of Jesus*, NTL (Philadelphia: Westminster, 1963); *Rediscovering the Teaching of Jesus* (New York: Harper & Row, 1967); "Wisdom and Apocalyptic in the Message of Jesus," in *SBLSP* 1972 (Missoula, Mont.: Scholars, 1972) 2.543–70; *The New Testament: An Introduction*, 288–99; "Eschatology and Hermeneutics," *JBL* 93 (1974) 3–14 (chap. 2 in this volume).

19. John Dominic Crossan, *In Parables: The Challenge of the Historical Jesus* (New York: Harper & Row, 1974). I am abbreviating my discussion of Crossan's work in *The New Testament: An Introduction*, 292–93. [Ed.] Crossan continued his work on the parables in subsequent works, principally: *The Dark Interval: Towards a Theology of Story* (Niles, Ill.: Argus, 1975; Sonoma, Calif.: Polebridge, 1988); *Finding Is the First Act: Trove Folktales and Jesus' Treasure Parable*, SemSt (Philadelphia: Fortress Press, 1979); and *Cliffs of Fall: Paradox and Polyvalence in the Parables of Jesus* (New York: Seabury, 1980).

20. Crossan, *In Parables*, 65–66.

21. Perrin, *The New Testament: An Introduction*, 295.

22. For further justification of this statement, see Perrin, *The New Testament: An Introduction*, 280–301.

23. A reasonably comprehensive presentation of the relevant material to 1964 by Ernst Staehelin, *Die Verkündigung des Reiches Gottes in der Kirche Jesu Christi: Zeugnisse aus allen Jahrhunderten und allen Konfessionen* (Basel: Reinhardt, 1951–65), takes up seven large volumes. It would be easy to compile a further volume to cover the last decade.

24. Paul Ricoeur, *The Symbolism of Evil*, trans. Emerson Buchanan (Boston: Beacon, 1969) 237.

25. *Symbolism of Evil*, 130.

26. *Symbolism of Evil*, 237.

27. *Symbolism of Evil*, 237.

28. We can support Ricoeur's point about what he calls "primordial symbols" by referring to Philip Wheelwright, who has a most important discussion

of symbols in his book *Metaphor and Reality*. Wheelwright defines a symbol as "a relatively stable and repeatable element of perceptual experience, standing for some larger meaning or set of meanings that cannot be given, or not fully given, in perceptual experience itself" (92). Concerning himself with literary symbols, Wheelwright speaks of five classes of symbols: (1) the presiding image of a single poem; (2) the personal symbol (one that "has continuing vitality and relevance for a poet's imaginative and perhaps actual life," 102); (3) symbols of ancestral vitality (symbols "lifted by one poet, for his own creative purposes, from earlier written sources" (105); (4) symbols of cultural range ("those which have a significant life for members of a community, of a cult, or of a larger secular or religious body," 108–9); (5) archetypal symbols ("those which carry the same or very similar meanings for a large portion, if not all, of mankind," 111). This graduation of symbols is extraordinarily suggestive; at the very least it challenges us to attempt something similar with regard to biblical symbols. For the moment, however, we simply note that in isolating "archetypal symbols" Wheelwright is calling attention to the class of symbols that Ricoeur calls "primordial symbols."

29. Ricoeur, *Symbolism of Evil*, 237.

30. Ricoeur, *Symbolism of Evil*, 239, italics added.

31. My quotations of Rauschenbusch are from *A Gospel for the Social Awakening: Selections from the Writings of Walter Rauschenbusch*, compiled by Benjamin E. Mays with an introduction by C. Howard Hopkins (New York: Association, 1950). This quotation is from p. 45.

32. Rauschenbusch, *A Gospel*, 14–15.

33. Rauschenbusch, *A Gospel*, 171–72.

34. This is my own translation of a passage from Bultmann's *Jesus* (1926) 46–47; see Perrin, "Eschatology and Hermeneutics," 7–8.

35. Perhaps the best statement of this in English is Bultmann, *Jesus Christ and Mythology* (New York: Scribners, 1958), originally written in English. Bultmann defined his hermeneutics in light of the general hermeneutical discussion in an important essay, "The Problem of Hermeneutics," in *New Testament and Mythology and Other Basic Writings*, ed. Schubert Ogden (Philadelphia: Fortress Press, 1984) 69–93. In this essay he defines his own position as being in the tradition of Schleiermacher and Dilthey (to which list he was later to add the English historian, R. G. Collingwood). See also Bultmann, *History and Eschatology: The Presence of Eternity*, Gifford Lectures 1955 (New York: Harper & Row, 1957).

36. A deliberate attempt to go beyond Bultmann in regard to hermeneutics is the so-called "New Hermeneutic" associated with the names of Ernst Fuchs and Gerhard Ebeling, and presented in English in James M. Robinson and John B. Cobb, eds., *The New Hermeneutic*, NFT 2 (New York: Harper & Row, 1964). This has proven of real interest to theological scholarship, but its rather narrow concentration upon "preaching texts" (Fuchs) and its rather hasty leap from language to "language event" without an adequate discussion of what it is about (certain kinds of language that make a "language event" possible) has tended to inhibit interest in it so far as the general discussion of hermeneutics is concerned. For all its title, it is perhaps more of a movement in contemporary theology than a contribution to contemporary hermeneutical theory.

37. In my "Eschatology and Hermeneutics" [chap. 2 in this volume], I reached a similar result by asking whether, in Philip Wheelwright's terms, Jesus used Kingdom of God as a "steno" or "tensive" symbol. On the basis of three considerations—Jesus' refusal to give a sign; his distinctive use of parables and proverbial sayings; and an exegesis of Luke 11:20; 17:20-21; Matt 11:12 (were I rewriting that essay today I would put less emphasis upon the first consideration and more upon the second and third)—I argued that Jesus used Kingdom of God as a tensive symbol. This means that, in the proclamation of Jesus, Kingdom of God does not have reference to "a single identifiable event which every man experiences at one and the same time," but rather "it is something which cannot be exhausted in any one event but which every man experiences in his own time" (3–14, esp. 13; 33 in this volume). Thus I reached an essentially Bultmannian position, but by way of a literary-critical understanding of the function of symbols rather than by a hermeneutics of "demythologizing."

2. Eschatology and Hermeneutics

[1.] Hans-Georg Gadamer, *Truth and Method,* trans. Garrett Barden and John Cumming (New York: Seabury, 1975); Paul Ricoeur, *Conflict in Interpretations: Essays in Hermeneutics,* Northwestern University Studies in Phenomenology and Existential Philosophy (Evanston, Ill.: Northwestern Univ. Press, 1974); Emilio Betti, *Teoria generale della interpretazione,* 2 vols. (Milan: Giuffrè, 1955); and E. D. Hirsch, *Validity in Interpretation* (New Haven: Yale Univ. Press, 1967).

2. Norman Perrin, *The Kingdom of God in the Teaching of Jesus,* NTL (Philadelphia: Westminster, 1963).

3. Norman Perrin, "Wisdom and Apocalyptic in the Message of Jesus," in *The Society of Biblical Literature One Hundred Eighth Annual Meeting Proceedings,* ed. Lane C. McGaughy (Missoula, Mont.: Society of Biblical Literature, 1972) 2.543–70.

4. Johannes Weiss, *Jesus' Proclamation of the Kingdom of God,* trans. Richard Hyde Hiers and David Larrimore Holland, LJS (Philadelphia: Fortress Press, 1971); 1st German ed. 1892; 2nd rev. German ed. 1900. See Perrin, *Kingdom,* 16–23.

[5.] Albert Schweitzer, *The Quest of the Historical Jesus,* 1st complete ed., trans. S. M. Cupitt, ed. John Bowden, FCBS (Minneapolis: Fortress Press, 2000).

6. "Die Kunstlehre des Verstehens schriftlich fixierter Lebensäusserungen"; Wilhelm Dilthey, quoted from Rudolf Bultmann, "The Problem of Hermeneutics," in *New Testament and Mythology and Other Basic Writings,* ed. Schubert Ogden (Philadelphia: Fortress Press, 1984) 69–93.

[7.] See two helpful articles by Bruce J. Malina: "Interpretation: Reading, Abduction, Metaphor," in *The Bible and the Politics of Exegesis: Essays in Honor of Norman K. Gottwald on His Sixty-fifth Birthday,* ed. David Jobling et al. (Cleveland: Pilgrim, 1991) 253–66 (+ 355–58); and idem, "Reading Theory Perspective: Reading Luke-Acts," in *The Social World of Luke-Acts: Models for Interpretation,* ed. Jerome H. Neyrey (Peabody, Mass.: Hendrickson, 1991) 3–23.

8. R. H. Hiers and D. L. Holland in Weiss, *Jesus' Proclamation*, 16.

9. Weiss, *Jesus' Proclamation*, 134–35.

10. Rudolf Bultmann, *Primitive Christianity in Its Contemporary Setting*, trans. Reginald H. Fuller (New York: World, 1956) 96–97.

11. Bultmann, *Primitive*, 87–88.

12. Bultmann, *Primitive*, 92.

13. Bultmann, *Jesus and the Word*, trans. Louise Pettibone Smith and Erminie Huntress Lantero (New York: Scribners, 1958) 51–52. [Ed.] Perrin discusses Bultmann's views at length in *The Kingdom of God in the Teaching of Jesus* (Philadelphia: Westminster, 1963) 112–29.

14. Perrin, *The Kingdom*, 116.

[15.] For current discussions of Phil 2:5-11, see Ralph P. Martin and Brian J. Dodd, eds., *Where Christology Began: Essays on Philippians 2* (Louisville: Westminster John Knox, 1998).

16. See, for example, *Rediscovering the Teaching of Jesus* (New York: Harper & Row, 1967) 22–23. [Ed.] For Käsemann's work see: Ernst Käsemann, "Sentences of Holy Law in the New Testament," in *New Testament Questions of Today*, trans. W. J. Montague (Philadelphia: Fortress Press, 1969) 66–81.

[17.] Perrin describes the consideration of genre, linguistic form, and function under the rubric "literary criticism"; but Old Testament scholars have long discussed these issues within the methodology of form criticism. See especially Klaus Koch, *The Growth of the Biblical Tradition: The Form-Critical Method*, trans. S. M. Cuppitt (New York: Scribners, 1969); and Rolf Knierim, "Criticism of Literary Features, Form, Tradition, and Redaction," in *The Hebrew Bible and Its Modern Interpreters*, ed. Douglas A. Knight and Gene M. Tucker (Philadelphia: Fortress Press, 1985) 123–65.

18. Norman Perrin, "Wisdom and Apocalyptic."

19. Philip Wheelwright, *Metaphor and Reality* (Bloomington: Indiana Univ. Press, 1962); and Paul Ricoeur, *The Symbolism of Evil*, trans. Emerson Buchanan (Boston: Beacon, 1969).

20. Ricoeur, *Symbolism*, 15.

21. Richard A. Edwards, *The Sign of Jonah in the Theology of the Evangelists and Q*, SBT 2/18 (Naperville, Ill.: Allenson, 1971). [Ed.] See also Simon Chow, *The Sign of Jonah Reconsidered: A Study of Its Meaning in the Gospel Traditions*, CBNT 27 (Stockholm: Almqvist & Wiksell, 1995).

3. Parables and Hermeneutics

1. Adolf Jülicher, *Die Gleichnisreden Jesu*, 2 vols. (Darmstadt: Wissenschaftliche Buchgesellschaft, 1963), vol. 1: 1st ed. 1888; 2nd ed. 1899; vol. 2: 1st ed. 1899; 2nd ed. 1910. [Ed.] See Ulrich Mell, editor, *Die Gleichnisreden Jesu 1899–1999: Beiträge zum Dialog mit Adolf Jülicher*, BZNW 103 (Berlin: de Gruyter, 1999); and William Baird, *The History of New Testament Research*, vol. 2: *From Jonathan Edwards to Rudolf Bultmann* (Minneapolis: Fortress Press, 2003) 156–62.

2. Jülicher, *Die Gleichnisreden Jesu*, 2.266.

3. Jülicher, *Die Gleichnisreden Jesu*, 2.276.

4. Jülicher, *Die Gleichnisreden Jesu*, 2.288.

5. Jülicher, *Die Gleichnisreden Jesu*, 2.432.

6. Jülicher, *Die Gleichnisreden Jesu*, 2.467.

7. Jülicher, *Die Gleichnisreden Jesu*, 2.536.

8. Jülicher, *Die Gleichnisreden Jesu*, 2.596.

9. Jülicher, *Die Gleichnisreden Jesu*, 1.182.

10. Jülicher, "Die Religion Jesu und die Anfänge des Christentums bis zum Nichaenum (325)," in *Die Christliche Religion: Mit Einschluss der israelitisch-jüdischen Religion*, ed. Julius Wellhausen and Adolf Jülicher, Die Kultur der Gegenwart 1.4 (Berlin: Teubner, 1906).

11. Joachim Jeremias, *The Parables of Jesus*, rev. ed., trans. S. H. Hooke (New York: Scribners, 1972). Since Jeremias constantly revises and rewrites his major books, one should note that the first German edition appeared in 1947 and that subsequent substantial revisions appeared in the 3rd (1954) and 6th (1963) German editions.

[12.] Albert Schweitzer, *The Quest of the Historical Jesus*, 1ˢᵗ complete edition, trans. Susan M. Cupitt and John Bowden, FCBS (Minneapolis: Fortress Press, 2000).

13. As Jeremias makes clear, he received the decisive impulse from C. H. Dodd, *The Parables of the Kingdom*, rev. ed. (New York: Scribners, 1961). Dodd's first edition was 1935.

14. Jeremias, *Parables*, 180.

15. Ernst Fuchs, "What Is Interpreted in the Exegesis of the New Testament?" in *Studies of the Historical Jesus*, trans. Andrew Scobie, SBT 1/42 (Naperville, Ill.: Allenson, 1964) 84–103. He dedicated this essay: "to Rudolf Bultmann on his seventy-fifth birthday."

16. Fuchs, "What Is Interpreted," 91–94.

17. Fuchs, "What Is Interpreted," 94–95.

18. Amos N. Wilder, *The Language of the Gospel: Early Christian Rhetoric* (New York: Harper & Row, 1964); reprinted as *Early Christian Rhetoric: The Language of the Gospel* (Cambridge: Harvard Univ. Press, 1971).

19. Wilder, *Language*, 93.

20. Wilder, *Language*, 80.

21. Wilder, *Language*, 84.

22. Wilder, *Language*, 92.

23. Wilder, *Language*, 93.

24. A term used by Robinson about Gerhard Ebeling, Fuchs's partner in the New Hermeneutic; see James M. Robinson, "Basic Shifts in German Theology," *Int* 16 (1962) 97 [76–97].

25. Wilder, *Language*, 93.

26. Robert W. Funk, *Language, Hermeneutic, and Word of God: The Problem of Language in the New Testament and Contemporary Theology* (New York: Harper & Row, 1966). [Ed.] See also idem, *Parables and Presence: Forms of the New Testament Tradition* (Philadelphia: Fortress Press, 1982); and idem, *The Poetics of Biblical Narrative* (Sonoma, Calif.: Polebridge, 1988).

27. Funk, *Language*, 159, 161.

28. Funk, *Language*, 190ff.

29. Funk, *Language*, 213.

30. Funk, *Language*, 214.

31. Funk, *Language*, 216.

32. Dan O. Via Jr., *The Parables: Their Literary and Existential Dimension* (Philadelphia: Fortress Press, 1967). See my very positive review of his work in *Int* 21 (1967) 465–69.

33. Via, *Parables*, 99.

34. Via, *Parables*, 122.

35. Via, *Parables*, 128, 154.

36. Via, *Parables*, 159.

4. The Evangelist as Author

[1.] David Friedrich Strauss, *Das Leben Jesu, kritisch bearbeitet*, 2 vols. (Tübingen: Osiander, 1835–36); *The Life of Jesus, Critically Examined*, trans. George Eliot, ed. Peter C. Hodgson (Philadelphia: Fortress Press, 1973).

[2.] William Wrede, *The Messianic Secret*, trans. J. C. G. Greig, LTT (Cambridge: Clarke, 1971).

[3.] See, for example: R. H. Lightfoot, *The Gospel Message of St. Mark* (Oxford: Clarendon, 1950); Frederick C. Grant, *The Gospels: Their Origin and Their Growth* (New York: Harper, 1957); and Burton Scott Easton, *The Gospel before the Gospels* (New York: Scribners, 1928).

[4.] Rudolf Bultmann, *The History of the Synoptic Tradition*, trans. John Marsh (New York: Harper & Row, 1963); and Martin Dibelius, *From Tradition to Gospel*, trans. Bertram Lee Woolf (New York: Scribners, 1935).

5. Martin Dibelius, "Style Criticism of the Book of Acts," in *Studies in the Acts of the Apostles*, trans. Mary Ling, ed. Heinrich Greeven (New York: Scribners, 1956) 1–25.

6. Dibelius, "The Speeches in Acts and Ancient Historiography," in *Studies in the Acts of the Apostles*, 148.

7. Ernst Haenchen, *The Acts of the Apostles: A Commentary*, trans. Bernard Noble and Gerald Shinn, rev. R. McL. Wilson (Philadelphia: Westminster, 1971).

[8.] See, for example, Eldon J. Epp, "Textual Criticism," in *The New Testament and Its Modern Interpreters*, ed. Eldon J. Epp and George W. MacRae (Philadelphia: Fortress Press, 1989) 75–126; and Schuyler Brown, "Philology," in *The New Testament and Its Modern Interpreters*, 127–47.

[9.] See, for example: Howard Clark Kee, "Synoptic Studies," in *The New Testament and Its Modern Interpreters*, 245–69; and John S. Kloppenborg Verbin, *Excavating Q: The History and Setting of the Sayings Gospel* (Minneapolis: Fortress Press, 2000) 11–54.

[10.] See, for example: Peter C. Hodgson, *The Formation of Historical Theology: A Study of Ferdinand Christian Baur*, MMT (New York: Harper & Row, 1966); William Baird, *The History of New Testament Research*, vol. 1: *From Deism to Tübingen* (Minneapolis: Fortress Press, 1992) 258–94.

[11.] See, for example: Ekkehard W. Stegemann and Wolfgang Stegemann, *The Jesus Movement: A History of Its First Century*, trans. O. C. Dean Jr. (Minneapolis: Fortress Press, 1999).

[12.] See Norman Perrin, "The Use of *(Para)didonai* in Connection with the Passion of Jesus," in *Der Ruf Jesu und die Antwort der Gemeinde: Festschrift für J. Jeremias zum 70. Geburtstag*, ed. E. Lohse (Göttingen: Vandenhoeck & Ruprecht, 1970) 204–12; reprinted with a Postscript in *A Modern Pilgrimage in New Testament Christology* (Philadelphia: Fortress Press, 1974) 94–103.

[13.] Norman Perrin, *The New Testament: An Introduction*, 1st ed. (New York: Harcourt Brace Jovanovich, 1973).

[14.] See Edgar V. McKnight, *What Is Form Criticism?* GBS (Philadelphia: Fortress Press, 1969); Klaus Berger, *Formgeschichte des Neuen Testaments* (Heidelberg: Quelle & Meyer, 1984); Edgar V. McKnight, "Form and Redaction Criticism," in *The New Testament and Its Modern Interpreters*, 149–74; and Vernon K. Robbins, "Form Criticism (NT)," in *ABD* 2:841–44.

[15.] Ernst Käsemann, "Sentences of Holy Law in the New Testament," in *New Testament Questions of Today*, trans. W. J. Montague (Philadelphia: Fortress Press, 1969) 66–81.

[16.] Redaction criticism: Norman Perrin, *What Is Redaction Criticism?* GBS (Philadelphia: Fortress Press, 1969); Carl R. Kazmierski, *Jesus, the Son of God: A Study of the Markan Tradition and Its Redaction by the Evangelist*, FzB 33 (Würzburg: Echter, 1979); Jerome H. Neyrey, *The Passion according to Luke: A Redaction Study of Luke's Soteriology*, ThInq (New York: Paulist, 1985); C. Clifton Black, *The Disciples according to Mark: Markan Redaction in Current Debate*, JSNTSup 27 (Sheffield: JSOT Press, 1989); Robert H. Stein, *Gospels and Tradition: Studies on Redaction Criticism of the Synoptic Gospels* (Grand Rapids: Baker, 1991).

[17.] Ernst Lohmeyer, *Das Evangelium des Markus*, KEK (Göttingen: Vandenhoeck & Ruprecht, 1937); and R. H. Lightfoot, *The Gospel Message of St. Mark*.

[18.] Benjamin W. Bacon, *Studies in Matthew* (New York: Holt, 1930).

[19.] Ernst Haenchen, *The Acts of the Apostles*, trans. Bernard Noble, Gerald Shinn, Hugh Anderson, and rev. by R. McL. Wilson (Philadelphia: Westminster, 1971).

[20.] Jack Dean Kingsbury, *The Parables of Jesus in Matthew 13: A Study in Redaction Criticism* (Richmond, Va.: John Knox, 1969); and William G. Thompson's *Matthew's Advice to a Divided Community, Mt. 17,22—18,35*, AnBib 44 (Rome: Biblical Institute Press, 1970).

[21.] Theodore J. Weeden, *Mark—Traditions in Conflict* (Philadelphia: Fortress Press, 1971); Henri Irénée Marrou, *A History of Education in Antiquity*, trans. George Lamb (New York: Sheed & Ward, 1956).

5. Interpretation of the Gospel of Mark

[1.] William Wrede, *Das Messias-Geheimnis in den Evangelien* (Göttingen: Vandenhoeck & Ruprecht, 1901); ET: *The Messianic Secret*, trans. J. C. G. Greig,

LTT (Cambridge: Clarke, 1971). On this topic, see Albert Schweitzer, *The Quest of the Historical Jesus*, 1ˢᵗ complete ed., trans. S. M. Cupitt, ed. John Bowden, FCBS (Minneapolis: Fortress Press, 2001) 303–14; James L. Blevins, *The Messianic Secret in Markan Research: 1901–1976* (Washington, D.C.: University Press of America, 1981); Christopher M. Tuckett, ed., *The Messianic Secret*, IRT 1 (Philadelphia: Fortress Press, 1983); Heikki Räisänen, *The "Messianic Secret" in Mark*, trans. C. M. Tuckett, SNTIW (Edinburgh: T. & T. Clark, 1990); and John J. Pilch, "Secrecy in the Mediterranean World: An Anthropological Perspective," *BTB* 24 (1994) 151–57. See also Perrin's additions in note 25 below.

[2.] Karl Ludwig Schmidt, *Der Rahmen der Geschichte Jesu: Literarkritische Untersuchungen zur ältesten Jesusüberlieferung* (Berlin: Trowitzsch, 1919). See David P. Moessner, "Schmidt, Karl Ludwig," in *DBI* 2.444–45.

[3.] Martin Dibelius, *From Tradition to Gospel*, trans. Bertram Lee Woolf (New York: Scribners, 1934) 2–4.

[4.] Rudolf Bultmann, *The History of the Synoptic Tradition*, trans. John Marsh (New York: Harper & Row, 1963) 350.

[5.] R. H. Lightfoot, *History and Interpretation in the Gospels*, Bampton Lectures 1934 (New York: Harper, 1935); *Locality and Doctrine in the Gospels* (London: Hodder, 1938); and *The Gospel Message of St. Mark* (Oxford: Clarendon, 1950). See also C. Clifton Black, "Lightfoot, Robert Henry," in *DBI* 2.77–78.

6. In *What Is Redaction Criticism?* GBS (Philadelphia: Fortress Press, 1969), I treated Lightfoot as a pioneer redaction critic. But today I think it more accurate to speak of him in terms of literary criticism, for reasons that will become apparent as I proceed.

7. A particularly important aspect of their work was the demonstration of the fact that the Gospel is directed toward the parousia in "Galilee," and that in this context Galilee is symbolic, not geographical. For a discussion and references, see Norman Perrin, "Towards an Interpretation of the Gospel of Mark," in *Christology and a Modern Pilgrimage*, ed. Hans Dieter Betz (Missoula: Scholars, 1974) 27–30.

[8.] D. E. Nineham, *The Gospel of Saint Mark*, PNTC (Harmondsworth: Pelican, 1963).

[9.] Ernst Lohmeyer, *Das Evangelium des Markus*, KEK (Göttingen: Vandenhoeck & Ruprecht, 1937).

[10.] Günther Bornkamm, Gerhard Barth, and Heinz Joachim Held, *Tradition and Interpretation in the Gospel of Matthew*, trans. Percy Scott, NTL (Philadelphia: Westminster, 1963).

[11.] Hans Conzelmann, *The Theology of St. Luke*, trans. Geoffrey Buswell (New York: Harper, 1961).

[12.] Willi Marxsen, *Mark the Evangelist: Studies on the Redaction History of the Gospel*, trans. James Boyce (Nashville: Abingdon, 1969).

13. Marxsen, *Mark*, 42.

14. Marxsen, *Mark*, 94.

15. Marxsen, *Mark*, 148.

16. Marxsen, *Mark*, 166, 189.

17. This geographic understanding of the references to Galilee in the Gospel is a very unsatisfactory aspect of Marxsen's interpretation of Mark. He had not

taken sufficient account of the work of Lightfoot and his followers in England. See note 7 above.

18. Perrin, *What Is Redaction Criticism?* 1.

19. This is Dan Via's phrase, from his review of my *The New Testament: An Introduction* (New York: Harcourt Brace Jovanovich, 1974) in *JR* 55 (1975) 456–61. He points out that this is what is happening in my work in that book. Via's very perceptive remarks in that review have influenced me strongly in the writing of this essay.

20. In this respect recent American work contrasts strongly with work in Germany since Marxsen. The recent German work has remained redaction-critical in the narrower sense, searching for pre-Markan tradition in order to observe Markan redaction of it, or it has sought an overall theological conception, like the Lukan Salvation History (*Heilsgeschichte*), that could provide the clue to the interpretation of the Gospel as a whole.

21. Eduard Schweizer, *The Good News according to Mark*, trans. John Steely (Richmond, Va.: John Knox, 1970).

22. I am thinking particularly of Theodore J. Weeden, *Mark—Traditions in Conflict* (Philadelphia: Fortress Press, 1971) 1–19; John R. Donahue, *Are You the Christ? The Trial Narrative in the Gospel of Mark*, SBLDS 10 (Missoula, Mont.: Scholars, 1973); Werner H. Kelber, ed., *The Passion in Mark: Studies on Mark 14–16* (Philadelphia: Fortress Press, 1976), which includes important methodological essays by Kelber and Donahue; Dan O. Via, *Kerygma and Comedy in the New Testament* (Philadelphia: Fortress Press, 1975); Norman Perrin, "The Christology of Mark: A Study in Methodology," *JR* 51 (1971) 173–87; idem, "The Evangelist as Author: Reflections on Method in the Study and Interpretation of the Synoptic Gospels and Acts," *BR* 17 (1972) 5–18 [chap. 4 in this volume].

23. **Aretalogy:** James M. Robinson and Helmut Koester, *Trajectories through Early Christianity* (Philadelphia: Fortress Press, 1971). **Old Testament:** Schweizer, *Mark.* **Apocalyptic:** Howard Clark Kee, *Jesus in History: An Approach to the Study of the Gospels* (New York: Harcourt Brace Jovanovich, 1970; 3rd ed. 1996); and Perrin, *The New Testament.* On the whole matter, see Via, *Kerygma and Comedy,* 95–97. [Ed.] On aretalogy, see now Gregory J. Riley, *One Jesus, Many Christs: How Jesus Inspired Not One True Christianity, but Many* (Minneapolis: Fortress Press, 2000).

24. Via, *Kerygma and Comedy,* 93.

25. **Messianic Secret:** Wrede, *The Messianic Secret.* The subsequent literature is overwhelming. Some of the more important recent discussions are T. Alec Burkill, *Mysterious Revelation* (Ithaca, N.Y.: Cornell Univ. Press, 1963); and in Christopher M. Tuckett, ed., *The Messianic Secret,* IRT 1 (Philadelphia: Fortress Press, 1983) the following essays: Georg Strecker, "The Theory of the Messianic Secret in Mark's Gospel"; Eduard Schweizer, "The Question of the Messianic Secret in Mark"; Ulrich Luz, "The Secrecy Motif and the Markan Christology"; and William C. Robinson Jr., "The Quest for Wrede's Secret Messiah"; H.-D. Knigge, "The Meaning of Mark," *Int* 22 (1968) 53–70; Dan O. Via, *Kerygma and Comedy,* 138–42. **Christology and Discipleship:** Weeden, *Mark*; and many others. **Eschatology:** Werner H. Kelber, *The Kingdom in Mark: A New Place and Time* (Philadelphia: Fortress Press, 1974). **Passion and Parousia:**

Perrin, "Towards an Interpretation of the Gospel of Mark," following Lightfoot and other British scholars.

26. It is generally held that the exception to this is the passion narrative, which is supposed to have existed as a connected narrative prior to Mark, perhaps even in several versions. Kelber and the contributors to *The Passion in Mark* are challenging this view by pointing to the extent of the Markan literary activity in the passion narrative and by arguing the dependence of Luke and John upon Mark in the passion narrative. [Ed.] See Burton L. Mack, *The Myth of Innocence: Mark and Christian Origins* (Philadelphia: Fortress Press, 1988) 247–312.

27. I am of course speaking of the surface or sequential structure of the Gospel, rather than of the deep structure that is the concern of a structuralist critic. [Ed.] On multiple forms of structure, see Stan Rummel, "Narrative Structures in the Ugaritic Texts," in *Ras Shamra Parallels*, vol. 3, ed. Stan Rummel, AnBib 51 (Rome: Pontifical Biblical Institute Press, 1981) 221–33 [221–332].

28. On Mark 14:61-62 and its retrospective and prospective functions, see my essay, "The High Priest's Question and Jesus' Answer (Mark 14:61-62)," in *The Passion in Mark*, 80–95. The observations concerning 6:1-6a I owe to Kim Dewey, a graduate student at the University of Chicago.

29. Enthusiasm for Weeden's work at the level of method does not, of course, necessarily carry with it agreement with his conclusions.

30. I recognize that this is a most inadequate statement with regard to Via's book, but space forbids more at the present time.

31. Another concern I am assuming is that for Mark's Greek vocabulary and style, and also one for his compositional techniques following the pioneering work of Lightfoot and Lohmeyer in that regard. These things are the bread and butter of contemporary interpretation of the Gospel.

6. THE CHRISTOLOGY OF MARK

1. Joachim Rohde, *Rediscovering the Teaching of the Evangelists*, NTL (Philadelphia: Westminster, 1969; German ed. 1962); and Norman Perrin, *What Is Redaction Criticism?* GBS (Philadelphia: Fortress Press, 1969).

2. Redaction critics uniformly accept the Two-Source Hypothesis of the Synoptic Gospels and regard the successful results of their work as an added substantiation of it. [Ed.] For a recent discussion of the Two-Source Hypothesis see John S. Kloppenborg Verbin, *Excavating Q: The History and Setting of the Sayings Gospel* (Minneapolis: Fortress Press, 2000) 11–54.

3. Both Rhode and I review this work in the books mentioned in note 1 above. Unfortunately there is as yet no full-scale presentation in English of the theology of Matthew and Luke as we now understand it in light of the work of redaction critics. Tragically, Hans Conzelmann, the leading redaction critic to work on Luke and the author of the breakthrough in connection with his Gospel, has treated the matter most inadequately in his recently published *Outline of the Theology of the New Testament* (New York: Harper & Row, 1969; 2nd German ed. 1967).

4. Eduard Schweizer, "Anmerkungen zur Theologie des Markus," in *Neotestamentica et Patristica: Eine Freundesgabe, Herrn Professor Dr. Oscar Cullmann zu seinem 60. Geburtstag überreicht,* NovTSup 6 (Leiden: Brill, 1962) 35–46; and Ulrich Luz, "The Secrecy Motif and the Markan Christology," in *The Messianic Secret,* ed. Christopher Tuckett, IRT 1 (Philadelphia: Fortress Press, 1983) 75–96. [Ed.] See also Schweizer, "Mark's Theological Achievement," in *The Interpretation of Mark,* ed. William Telford, IRT 7 (Philadelphia: Fortress Press, 1985) 42–63.

5. Erich Grässer, "Jesus in Nazareth (Mark VI.1-6a): Notes on the Redaction and Theology of St. Mark," *NTS* 16 (1969–70) 1–23; and Johannes Schreiber, "Die Christologie des Markusevangeliums," *ZTK* 58 (1961) 261–68; and idem, *Die Theologie des Vertrauens: Eine redaktionsgeschichtliche Untersuchung des Markusevangeliums* (Hamburg: Furche, 1967). [Ed.] See also Schreiber, *Die Markuspassion: Eine redaktionsgeschichtliche Untersuchung,* BZNW 68 (Berlin: de Gruyter, 1993).

6. Etienne Trocmé, *The Formation of the Gospel according to Mark,* trans. Pamela Gaughan (Philadelphia: Westminster, 1975), French ed. 1963.

7. Ernst Lohmeyer, *Das Evangelium des Markus,* KEK (Göttingen: Vandenhoeck & Ruprecht, 1937); R. H. Lightfoot, *History and Interpretation in the Gospels* (New York: Harper, 1935); idem, *Locality and Doctrine in the Gospels* (London: Hodder, 1938); idem, *The Gospel Message of St. Mark* (Oxford: Clarendon, 1950; paperback ed. 1962). Two recent works by English scholars embodying this approach are: T. Alec Burkill, *Mysterious Revelation: An Examination of the Philosophy of St. Mark's Gospel* (Ithaca, N.Y.: Cornell Univ. Press, 1963); and D. E. Nineham, *The Gospel of Saint Mark,* PNTC (Harmondsworth: Pelican, 1963).

8. Leander E. Keck, "Mark 3:7-12 and Mark's Christology," *JBL* 84 (1965) 341–58.

9. See Norman Perrin, "The Creative Use of the Son of Man Traditions by Mark," *USQR* 23 (1967–68) 237–65; reprinted in *A Modern Pilgrimage in New Testament Christology* (Minneapolis: Fortress Press, 1974) 84–93.

10. Martin Kähler, *The So-called Historical Jesus and the Historic, Biblical Christ,* ed. and trans. Carl E. Braaten, Seminar Editions (Philadelphia: Fortress Press, 1964), 275.

11. Morton Smith, "Prolegomena to a Discussion of Aretalogies, Divine Men, the Gospels and Jesus," *JBL* 90 (1971) 174–99; and Moses Hadas and Morton Smith, *Heroes and Gods: Spiritual Biographies in Antiquity,* RelPer 13 (New York: Harper & Row, 1965). [Ed.] See Gregory J. Riley, *One Jesus, Many Christs: How Jesus Inspired Not One True Christianity, but Many* (Minneapolis: Fortress Press, 2000).

12. Howard Clark Kee, *Aretalogies, Hellenistic "Lives," and the Sources of Mark,* Colloquy Center for Hermeneutical Studies in Hellenistic and Modern Culture 12 (Berkeley: Center for Hermeneutical Studies, 1975); compare Kee, *Jesus in History: An Approach to the Study of the Gospels,* 2nd ed. (New York: Harcourt Brace Jovanovich, 1977) 121–65.

13. It goes without saying that considerations of model/purpose and of literary criticism will be helpful in the case of Matthew and Luke also. But

their model is Mark, so even here their redaction of Mark will be the indispensable key.

14. John R. Donahue, S.J., a student of mine working on the trial narrative, presented to the Catholic Biblical Association meeting in the summer of 1970 the following evidence of Markan literary activity in the narrative: (1) the use of the impersonal third person plural in introductory sentences with Jesus as the object of a verb in the same context; *kai* as parataxis compound of *erchomai*; the historic present; use of *pas* or *holos* to *universalize* a scene (twenty instances of this in Mark); (2) sentence with the order *kai*–participle–subject; tautologous repetition of key words or phrases as in Mark 14:56 and 59 (forty-seven instances of this in Mark) as "a Markan insertion technique" (Donahue's own discovery); and more. See now Donahue's *Are You the Christ? The Trial Narrative in the Gospel of Mark*, SBLDS 10 (Missoula, Mont.: Society of Biblical Literature, 1973). [Ed.] See also Donahue and Daniel J. Harrington, *Mark*, SacPag 2 (Collegeville, Minn.: Liturgical, 2002).

15. I quote the RSV but use "Son of Man" rather than the "Son of man" of that version.

16. The parallelism between Mark 8:31—9:1; 9:31-37; 10:32-45 (passion prediction—misunderstanding—teaching) shows that everything in the pericope after verse 31 is Markan. Moreover, the passion prediction itself is a Markan composition (as I shall argue later in this paper), and the teaching in verses 8:34—9:1 has been heavily edited and in part actually composed by Mark (see Norman Perrin, *What Is Redaction Criticism?* 44–51).

17. Perrin, *What Is Redaction Criticism?* 53–56. Theodore J. Weeden's work, which was a catalytic agent for me in this matter, has now been summarized in an article, "The Heresy that Necessitated Mark's Gospel," *ZNW* 59 (1968) 145–58; and also in his book, *Mark—Traditions in Conflict* (Philadelphia: Fortress Press, 1971).

18. This is important in the context of the fact that nowhere in the Gospels is Son of Man found except on the lips of Jesus (for one possible exception, see note 25 below). It is often argued on this basis that Jesus did use the term as a self-designation, and the tradition has remained true to him in this regard. The fact does, however, admit of an alternative explanation, admittedly more complex. In the first place, Son of Man is not a christological title. It is rather a designation for Jesus in his apocalyptic authority, derived from Daniel 7 and then used in the paradox of the necessity for his passion ("the Son of Man goes as it is written of him . . . is betrayed"; Mark 14:21). It is never used confessionally and it tended not to survive the movement of the church into the Greek-speaking world. Compare the formula in 1 Thess 1:10, where Jesus is expected from heaven as Son of God, not Son of Man. In the Hellenized version of Mark 10:45 found in 1 Tim 2:5, it is not the Son of Man, but "the man Christ Jesus" who gave himself as a ransom for all. In the Synoptic tradition before Mark, all the sayings are in the form of words of Jesus, including the Son of Man sayings. Mark develops the use of Son of Man very extensively, as we shall argue below, but he has the convention of restricting it, the true Christology, to the lips of Jesus. Luke never uses the expression except in dependence upon a source, and the additional uses by Matthew and John are not extensive enough to

break the conventions of the Synoptic tradition and of Mark, especially in view of the total absence of any confessional use of Son of Man as a christological title. So it is possible to account for the evidence in the Gospels without recourse to the hypothesis that Jesus used the expression as a self-designation in a way more meaningful than in an idiomatic expression such as "the Son of Man came eating and drinking," where it seems to be simply a circumlocution whereby the speaker refers to himself. See Perrin, "The Son of Man in the Synoptic Tradition," *BR* 13 (1968) 1–23; reprinted with an additional Postscript in *A Modern Pilgrimage in New Testament Christology*, 57–83.

19. A student of mine investigated the summaries from the viewpoint of Mark's Christology: Vernon K. Robbins, "The Christology of Mark" (Ph.D. diss., Univ. of Chicago Divinity School, 1969). [Ed.] See also idem, *Jesus the Teacher: A Socio-Rhetorical Interpretation of Mark* (Philadelphia: Fortress Press, 1984); and Robbins and David B. Gowler, *New Boundaries in Old Territory: Form and Social Rhetoric in Mark*, ESEC 3 (New York: Lang, 1994).

20. See Keck, "Mark 3:7-12"; and compare Robbins, "Christology," 77–103, where Keck's insights are taken up and developed further.

21. Keck, "Mark 3:7-12," 358. More recently, Paul J. Achtemeier has published the first part of an extended study of the pre-Markan tradition of miracle stories and its use by the Evangelist in his "Towards the Isolation of Pre-Markan Miracle Catenae," *JBL* 89 (1970) 265–91. He argues for a rather different analysis of the pre-Markan material, seeing two cycles of stories (catenae), as does Keck, but claiming that they are symmetrical, with each including a sea miracle, three healings, and a feeding. Catena I is Mark 4:35—5:43; 6:34-44, 53; and Catena II is Mark 6:45-51; 8:22-26; 7:24b-30, 33-37; 8:1-10. I find myself in agreement with many of Achtemeier's observations. But I have three reservations about this division. In the first place, such symmetry is itself suspicious. Then, second, the second group of three healings (the Blind Man at Bethsaida [8:22-26], the Syrophoenician Woman [7:24b-30], and the Deaf Mute [7:32-37] is not homogeneous. The first and third exhibit a common concern for healing techniques, but the second has the same aura of healing by fiat that is characteristic of Achtemeier's Catena I (the Gerasene Demoniac [5:1-20], the Woman with the Hemorrhage [5:25-34], Jairus's Daughter [5:21-23, 35-43]). Last, Keck's argument about the relationship with the subsequent cycle of stories is an important factor. Publication of the remaining parts of Achtemeier's study may change the situation, but at the moment I am personally inclined to stay with Keck's analysis and conclusion, except that I would add the Syrophoenician Woman to his cycle of miracle stories originally presenting Jesus as a divine man (*theios anēr*) and now being reinterpreted by Mark. [Ed.] See Achtemeier, "The Origin and Function of the Pre-Markan Miracle Catenae," *JBL* 91 (1972) 198–221; and idem, "Miracles and the Historical Jesus: A Study of Mark 9:14-29," *CBQ* 37 (1975) 471–91.

22. Even if this reference should be of real significance for an understanding of the historical occasion for the writing of Mark, it is not a significant reference in terms of the Markan Christology. That the reference is of real significance for the historical understanding of Mark has been strongly argued by a student of mine, Werner H. Kelber in his "Kingdom and Parousia

in the Gospel of Mark" (Ph.D. diss., Univ. of Chicago Divinity School, 1970) 151–59. This work in revised form is published as *The Kingdom in Mark: A New Place and a New Time* (Philadelphia: Fortress Press, 1974).

23. In view of the importance of this title in Mark, one is tempted to say that if it was not part of the original superscription it should have been; and the scribe who first added it was Markan in purpose if not in name!

24. A point I expect to argue in some detail in a subsequent publication, *Towards the Interpretation of the Gospel of Mark.* [Ed.] Perrin did not complete this work before his death.

25. See Perrin, "The Creative Use." The point that 2:10 is Markan can now be strengthened by two further observations. The first of these is the anacoluthon that makes the Son of Man reference read very like a comment by the Evangelist addressing his readers, rather as he does in 13:14. Joseph A. Fitzmyer suggested to me verbally that this may be one instance where Son of Man is not on the lips of Jesus in the Gospel. The second is that the tautological repetition of the command to the paralytic may indicate that we have here an example of the Markan insertion technique identified by John R. Donahue (see note 14 above).

26. See Perrin, *Rediscovering the Teaching of Jesus* (New York: Harper & Row, 1967) 173–85, 185–91.

27. This last conclusion received strong support in Matthew Black's presidential address to the Society for New Testament Studies in August 1970, where he demonstrated the strong evidence that now exists for such a use of the Old Testament by early Christians in the development of Kyrios, Son of God, and Son of Man Christologies. The address has been published as "The Christological Use of the Old Testament in the New Testament," *NTS* 18 (1971–72) 1–14.

28. I propose to discuss these problems in detail in the subsequent publication referred to in note 24 above.

29. Eduard Lohse, *Märtyrer und Gottesknecht*, FRLANT 64 (Göttingen: Vandenhoeck & Ruprecht, 1955).

30. Frederick Houk Borsch, *The Christian and Gnostic Son of Man*, SBT 2/14 (Naperville, Ill.: Allenson, 1970) 23–26, with reference to earlier literature.

31. Heinz Eduard Tödt, *The Son of Man in the Synoptic Tradition*, trans. Dorothea M. Barton, NTL (Philadelphia: Westminster, 1965) 202–11. The ransom clause actually comes from a well-defined tradition in the early church in which *(para)didonai* is used of the passion. I have isolated and discussed that tradition in an article published in a Festschrift for my *Doktorvater*, Joachim Jeremias. Norman Perrin, "The Use of *(Para)didonai* in Connection with the Passion of Jesus," in *Der Ruf Jesu und die Antwort der Gemeinde: Festschrift für J. Jeremias zum 70. Geburtstag*, ed. Eduard Lohse (Göttingen: Vandenhoeck & Ruprecht, 1970) 204–12; reprinted with a Postscript in *A Modern Pilgrimage in New Testament Christology*, 94–103.

32. For the justification of this and subsequent statements about the use of *(para)didonai* in the tradition, see Perrin, "The Use of *(Para)didonai.*"

33. Tödt, *Son of Man*, 152–221; Ferdinand Hahn, *The Titles of Jesus in Christology: Their History in Early Christianity*, trans. Harold Knight and George

Ogg (New York: World, 1969) 37–42; Georg Strecker, "The Passion and Resurrection Predictions in Mark's Gospel," *Int* 22 (1968) 421–42.

34. This, too, will be argued in the subsequent publication referred to in note 24 above, on the basis that (1) the verbal parallelism of the last part of the predictions indicates a common origin; (2) there is no known setting in life (*Sitz im Leben*) for them as units apart from their setting in the Gospel of Mark (*Sitz im Evangelium des Markus*); and (3) that there is evidence for the prior existence of their separate parts in the tradition of the church.

7. JESUS AND THE THEOLOGY OF THE NEW TESTAMENT

1. Werner Georg Kümmel, *Theology of the New Testament according to Its Major Witnesses: Jesus–Paul–John*, trans. J. E. Steely (Nashville: Abingdon, 1973).

2. Rudolf Bultmann, *Theology of the New Testament*, trans. K. Grobel, 2 vols. (New York: Scribners, 1951–55) 1.3; Hans Conzelmann, *An Outline of New Testament Theology*, trans. John Bowden (New York: Harper & Row, 1969) xvii.

3. Joachim Jeremias, *New Testament Theology*, vol. 1: *The Proclamation of Jesus*, trans. John Bowden (New York: Scribners, 1971). At Jeremias's death in 1981 the second volume had not appeared. Leonhard Goppelt, *Theologie des Neuen Testament*, ed. Jürgen Roloff (Göttingen: Vandenhoeck & Ruprecht, 1975–76); vol. 1: *Theology of the New Testament: The Ministry of Jesus in Its Theological Significance*, ed. Jürgen Roloff, trans. John E. Alsup (Grand Rapids: Eerdmans, 1981).

4. Perrin, *The New Testament: An Introduction. Proclamation and Parenesis, Myth and History* (New York: Harcourt Brace Jovanovich, 1974); 2nd ed. revised and co-authored with Dennis C. Duling, 1982; 3rd ed. Duling and Perrin, 1994; 4th ed. Duling, 2003.

5. Perrin, *Rediscovering the Teaching of Jesus* (New York: Harper & Row, 1967); Van A. Harvey, *The Historian and the Believer* (New York: Macmillan, 1966).

6. Erich Grässer, "Motive und Methoden der neueren Jesus-Literatur: An Beispielen dargestellt," *VF* 18 (1973) 3–45, esp. 18, 43–44; and idem, "Der Mensch Jesus als Thema der Theologie," in *Jesus und Paulus: Festschrift für Werner Georg Kümmel zum 70. Geburtstag*, ed. E. Earl Ellis and Erich Grässer, 2nd ed. (Göttingen: Vandenhoeck & Ruprecht, 1978) 129–50, esp. 148.

7. Perrin, *Jesus and the Language of the Kingdom: Symbol and Metaphor in New Testament Interpretation* (Philadelphia: Fortress Press, 1976).

8. Perrin, "Eschatology and Hermeneutics: Reflections on Method in the Interpretation of the New Testament," *JBL* 93 (1974) 3–14; [Ed.] now chap. 2 in this volume.

9. Richard A. Edwards, *A Theology of Q: Eschatology, Prophecy, Wisdom* (Philadelphia: Fortress Press, 1976). [Ed.] For the most recent study of Q's theology, see John S. Kloppenborg Verbin, *Excavating Q: The History and Setting of the Sayings Gospel* (Minneapolis: Fortress Press, 2000) 353–408.

10. Chapter 4 of Perrin, *Introduction*, is titled "Apocalyptic Christianity."

[11.] On the Son of Man traditions, see Walter Wink, *The Human Being: Jesus and the Son of the Man* (Minneapolis: Fortress Press, 2001).

12. Perrin, *Introduction*, 190–91.

13. Hans Conzelmann, *The Theology of St. Luke*, trans. G. Buswell (Philadelphia: Fortress Press, 1961) esp. 17–206.

14. Perrin, *Introduction*, 217–19.

[15.] For both the history of scholarship and contemporary discussions of historical Jesus research, see the select bibliography on pp. 140–41 in this volume.

[16.] For a new translation and commentary on 1 *Enoch*, see George W. E. Nickelsburg, *1 Enoch 1*, Hermeneia (Minneapolis: Fortress Press, 2001); and Nickelsburg and James VanderKam, *1 Enoch 2*, Hermeneia (Minneapolis: Fortress Press, forthcoming).

[17.] For a discussion of the importance of this essay, see Dan O. Via, *What Is New Testament Theology?* GBS (Minneapolis: Fortress Press, 2002) 13–14.

8. THE CHALLENGE OF NEW TESTAMENT THEOLOGY

1. Throughout the paper I use the expression "New Testament theology" (as are such expressions as "systematic theology" or "constructive theology") to denote an aspect of theological study and discussion.

2. Martin Kähler, *The So-called Historical Jesus and the Historic, Biblical Christ*, ed. and trans. Carl E. Braaten, Seminar Editions (Philadelphia: Fortress Press, 1964).

3. Rudolf Bultmann, *Jesus and the Word*, trans. Louise Pettibone Smith and Erminie Huntress Lantero (New York: Scribners, 1958); idem, *Theology of the New Testament*, vol. 1, trans. Kendrick Grobel (New York: Scribners, 1951); idem, *Primitive Christianity in Its Contemporary Setting*, trans. R. H. Fuller (New York: Meridian, 1956); idem, "The Primitive Christian Kerygma and the Historical Jesus," in *The Historical Jesus and the Kerygmatic Christ*, ed. Carl E. Braaten and Roy A. Harrisville (New York: Abingdon, 1964).

4. Norman Perrin, *The Kingdom of God in the Teaching of Jesus*, NTL (Philadelphia: Westminster, 1963).

5. Gotthold Hasenhüttl, *Der Glaubensvollzug: Eine Begegnung mit Rudolf Bultmann aus katholischem Glaubens-Verständnis*, Koinonia 1 (Essen: Ludgerus, 1963).

6. Rudolf Bultmann, *History of the Synoptic Tradition*, trans. John Marsh (New York: Harper & Row, 1963); idem, *Form Criticism*, trans. Frederick C. Grant (New York: Harper & Row, 1962).

7. Rudolf Bultmann, *History and Eschatology*, Gifford Lectures 1955 (New York: Harper, 1957). The U.S. edition was also published as *The Presence of Eternity*.

8. James M. Robinson, "The New Hermeneutic at Work," *Int* 18 (1964) 347–59, esp. 358.

9. Rudolf Bultmann, *Kerygma and Myth: A Theological Debate*, rev. ed., ed. Hans-Werner Bartsch, trans. R. H. Fuller (New York: Harper & Row, 1961) 117.

10. Joachim Jeremias, "The Search for the Historical Jesus," in *Jesus and the Message of the New Testament*, ed. K. C. Hanson, FCBS (Minneapolis: Fortress Press, 2002) 1–17.

11. Karl Jaspers and Rudolf Bultmann, *Myth and Christianity: An Inquiry into the Possibility of Religion without Myth* (New York: Noonday, 1958). Bultmann's later rejoinder is his essay, "Das Befremdliche des christlichen Glaubens," *ZTK* 55 (1958) 185–200.

12. Robinson coined the phrase as the title of a book in which he presented and interpreted the discussion to English language readers: James M. Robinson, *A New Quest of the Historical Jesus*, SBT 1/25 (Naperville, Ill.: Allenson, 1959).

13. Ernst Käsemann, "The Problem of the Historical Jesus," in *Essays on New Testament Themes*, SBT 1/41 (Naperville, Ill.: Allenson, 1964) 15–47.

14. Particularly interesting here is the work of Günther Bornkamm and his students in Heidelberg: Günther Bornkamm, Gerhard Barth, and Heinz Joachim Held, *Tradition and Interpretation in the Gospel of Matthew*, trans. Percy Scott, NTL (Philadelphia: Westminster, 1963); Heinz Eduard Tödt, *The Son of Man in the Synoptic Tradition*, trans. Dorothea M. Barton (Philadelphia: Westminster, 1965); and Ferdinand Hahn, *The Titles of Jesus in Christology: Their History in Early Christianity*, trans. Harold Knight and George Ogg (New York: World, 1969). Ernst Käsemann himself has done significant work here also, particularly in "Sentences of Holy Law in New Testament," in *New Testament Questions of Today*, trans. W. J. Montague (Philadelphia: Fortress Press, 1969) 66–81; idem, "The Beginning of Christian Theology," in *New Testament Questions of Today*, 82–107; idem, "On the Subject of Primitive Christian Apocalyptic," in *New Testament Questions of Today*, 108–37.

15. Herbert Braun, "Significance of Qumran for the Problem of the Historical Jesus," in *The Historical Jesus and the Kerygmatic Christ*, ed. Carl E. Braaten and Roy A. Harrisville (New York: Abingdon, 1964) 69–78.

16. James M. Robinson, *A New Quest;* idem, "The Formal Structure of Jesus' Message," in *Current Issues in New Testament Interpretation: Essays in Honor of Otto A. Piper*, ed. William Klassen and Graydon F. Snyder (New York: Harper, 1962) 91–110; idem, "The Recent Debate on the New Quest," *JBR* 30 (1962) 198–208.

17. Ernst Fuchs, *Studies of the Historical Jesus*, trans. Andrew Scobie, SBT 1/42 (Naperville, Ill.: Allenson, 1964).

18. Gerhard Ebeling, *The Nature of Faith*, trans. Ronald Gregor Smith (Philadelphia: Fortress Press, 1961); idem, *Word and Faith*, trans. James W. Leitch (Philadelphia: Fortress Press, 1963); idem, *Theology and Proclamation: A Discussion with Rudolf Bultmann*, trans. John Riches (Philadelphia, Fortress Press, 1966).

19. John B. Cobb Jr. and James M. Robinson, eds., *The New Hermeneutic*, NFT 2 (New York: Harper & Row, 1964).

20. See Bultmann's essay, "The Primitive Christian Kerygma and the Historical Jesus," esp. 33.

21. In Ebeling's *Theology and Proclamation*, 32–93, 124–30.

22. A brief selection from the more important literature on this question is as follows: Bultmann, *Kerygma and Myth;* idem, *Kerygma and History;* Carl E. Braaten and Roy A. Harrisville, eds., *Kerygma and History: A Symposium on the Theology of Rudolf Bultmann* (Nashville: Abingdon, 1962); and Günther Bornkamm, "Die Theologie Rudolf Bultmanns in der neueren Diskussion," *TRu* 29 (1963–64) 33–141.

23. We are now following Bultmann's original essay, "New Testament and Mythology," in *New Testament Mythology and Other Basic Writings,* ed. and trans. Schubert M. Ogden (Philadelphia: Fortress, 1984) 1–43.

24. Compare Bornkamm, "Die Theologie Rudolf Bultmanns," esp. 124–41.

25. Karl Barth, "Rudolf Bultmann—An Attempt to Understand Him," in *Kerygma and Myth,* vol. 2, 83–132.

26. Jaspers and Bultmann, *Myth and Christianity.* See also Hans-Werner Bartsch, "Bultmann and Jaspers," in *Kerygma and Myth,* vol. 2, 195–215.

27. Schubert Ogden, *Christ without Myth* (New York: Harper, 1961).

28. Compare Fuchs, *Studies of the Historical Jesus;* Ebeling, *The Nature of Faith;* Cobb and Robinson, eds., *The New Hermeneutic;* and two reviews by Robinson: "Neo-Liberalism," *Int* 15 (1961) 484–91; and "The New Hermeneutic at Work," *Int* 18 (1964) 347–59.

29. Langdon Gilkey, *Naming the Whirlwind: The Renewal of God-Language* (Indianapolis: Bobbs-Merrill, 1969).

Bibliography

Norman Perrin's Major Works

1963   *The Kingdom of God in the Teaching of Jesus.* NTL. Philadelphia: Westminster.

1967   *Rediscovering the Teaching of Jesus.* New York: Harper & Row. (Paperback ed. with new Preface, 1976.)

1969   *The Promise of Bultmann: The Promise of Theology.* Edited by Martin Marty. Philadelphia: Lippincott. (Reprinted Philadelphia: Fortress Press, 1979.)

1969   *What Is Redaction Criticism?* GBS. Philadelphia: Fortress Press.

1974   *The New Testament: An Introduction. Proclamation and Parenesis, Myth and History.* New York: Harcourt Brace Jovanovich.

1974   *A Modern Pilgrimage in New Testament Christology.* Philadelphia: Fortress Press.

1976   *Jesus and the Language of the Kingdom: Symbol and Metaphor in New Testament Interpretation.* Philadelphia: Fortress Press.

1977   *The Resurrection according to Matthew, Mark, and Luke.* Philadelphia: Fortress Press.

Assessments of Norman Perrin's Work

Chilton, Bruce. "The Kingdom of God and the Historical Norman Perrin." *Criterion* 37 (1998) 18–23.

Donahue, John R. "A Pilgrimage Interrupted: Norman Perrin's Unfolding New Testament Theology." *Criterion* 37 (1998) 24–28.

———. "Norman Perrin." In *DBI* 2.264–65.

Duling, Dennis C. "Introductory Biographical Sketch." *Criterion* 37 (1998) 16.

———. "Norman Perrin and the Kingdom of God: Review and Response." *JR* 64 (1984) 468–83.

———, and M. Santiago. "Norman Perrin (1920–1976): A Tribute." Perrin Memorial Session, SBL Annual Meeting, 1996. 13-minute video.

Epp, Eldon J. "Norman Perrin on the Kingdom of God." In *Christology and a Modern Pilgrimage: A Discussion with Norman Perrin,* edited by Hans Dieter Betz, 75–80. Rev. ed. Missoula, Mont.: Society of Biblical Literature, 1974.

Furnish, Victor P. "Notes on a Pilgrimage: Norman Perrin and New Testament Christology." In *Christology and a Modern Pilgrimage: A Discussion with Norman Perrin,* edited by Hans Dieter Betz, 61–73. Rev. ed. Missoula, Mont.: Society of Biblical Literature, 1974.

Grässer, Erich. "Norman Perrin's Contribution to the Question of the Historical Jesus." *JR* 64 (1984) 484–500.

Hobbs, E. C. "Norman Perrin on Methodology in the Interpretation of Mark." In *Christology and a Modern Pilgrimage: A Discussion with Norman Perrin,* edited by Hans Dieter Betz, 53–60. Rev. ed. Missoula, Mont.: Society of Biblical Literature, 1974.

Kelber, Werner H. "Remembering Norman Perrin." *Criterion* 37 (1998) 29–33.

———. "The Work of Norman Perrin: An Intellectual Pilgrimage." *JR* 64 (1984) 452–67.

Koester, Helmut. "The Historical Jesus: Some Comments and Thoughts on Norman Perrin's *Rediscovering the Teaching of Jesus*." In *Christology and a Modern Pilgrimage: A Discussion with Norman Perrin,* edited by Hans Dieter Betz, 81–89. Rev. ed. Missoula, Mont.: Society of Biblical Literature, 1974.

Mercer, Calvin R. *Norman Perrin's Interpretation of the New Testament: From "Exegetical Method" to "Hermeneutical Process."* SABH 2. Mercer, Ga.: Mercer Univ. Press, 1986.

———. "Norman Perrin's Pilgrimage: Releasing the Bible to the Public." *ChrCen* 103 (1986) 483–86.

Ricoeur, Paul. "From Proclamation to Narrative." *JR* 64 (1984) 501–12.

Robinson, James M. "*The Promise of Bultmann.*" In *Christology and a Modern Pilgrimage: A Discussion with Norman Perrin,* edited by Hans Dieter Betz, 97–100. Rev. ed. Missoula, Mont.: Society of Biblical Literature, 1974.

Seal, W. O. "Norman Perrin and His 'School': Retracing a Pilgrimage." *JSNT* 20 (1984) 87–107.

Wilder, Amos. "Norman Perrin and the Relation of Historical Knowledge to Faith." *HTR* 82 (1989) 201–11.

———. "Norman Perrin, *What Is Redaction Criticism?*" In *Christology and a Modern Pilgrimage: A Discussion with Norman Perrin,* edited by Hans Dieter Betz, 91–96. Rev. ed. Missoula, Mont.: Society of Biblical Literature, 1974.

SELECT BIBLIOGRAPHY ON THE HISTORICAL JESUS

Allison, Dale C. *Jesus of Nazareth: Millenarian Prophet.* Minneapolis: Fortress Press, 1998.

Borg, Marcus. *Jesus in Contemporary Scholarship.* Valley Forge, Pa.: Trinity Press International, 1994.

———. *Meeting Jesus Again for the First Time: The Historical Jesus and the Heart of Contemporary Faith.* San Francisco: HarperSanFrancisco, 1994.

Chilton, Bruce, and Craig A. Evans, editors. *Authenticating the Activities of Jesus.* NTTS 28.2. Leiden: Brill, 1999.

———. *Authenticating the Words of Jesus.* NTTS 28.1. Leiden: Brill, 1999.

———. *Studying the Historical Jesus: Evaluations of the State of Current Research.* NTTS 19. Leiden: Brill, 1994.

Crossan, John Dominic. *The Historical Jesus: The Life of a Mediterranean Jewish Peasant.* San Francisco: HarperSanFrancisco, 1991.

———. *Jesus: A Revolutionary Biography.* San Francisco: HarperSanFrancisco, 1994.

Crossan, John Dominic, and Jonathan L. Reed. *Excavating Jesus: Beneath the Stones, beneath the Texts*. San Francisco: HarperSanFrancisco, 2001.

Duling, Dennis C. *Jesus Christ through History*. New York: Harcourt Brace Jovanovich, 1979.

Herzog, William R. II. *Jesus, Justice, and the Reign of God: A Ministry of Liberation*. Louisville: Westminster John Knox, 2000.

Horsley, Richard A. *Jesus and Empire: The Kingdom of God and the New World Order*. Minneapolis: Fortress Press, 2003.

———. *Jesus and the Spiral of Violence: Popular Jewish Resistance in Roman Palestine*. San Francisco: Harper & Row, 1987. Reprinted Minneapolis: Fortress Press, 1993.

Horsley, Richard A., and Neil Asher Silberman. *The Message and the Kingdom: How Jesus and Paul Ignited a Revolution and Transformed the Ancient World*. Minneapolis: Fortress Press, 2002 [1997].

Jeremias, Joachim. *Jesus and the Message of the New Testament*. FCBS. Minneapolis: Fortress Press, 2002.

Käsemann, Ernst. "The Problem of the Historical Jesus." In *Essays on New Testament Themes*, 15–47. SBT 1/41. Naperville, Ill.: Allenson, 1964.

Keck, Leander A. *Who Is Jesus? History in the Present Tense*. SPNT. Minneapolis: Fortress Press, 2001.

Malina, Bruce J. *The Social Gospel of Jesus: The Kingdom of God in Mediterranean Perspective*. Minneapolis: Fortress Press, 2001.

Oakman, Douglas E. "The Archaeology of First-Century Galilee and the Social Interpretation of the Historical Jesus." In *SBL 1994 Seminar Papers*, 220–51. Atlanta: Scholars, 1994.

———. *Jesus and the Economic Questions of His Day*. Studies in the Bible and Early Christianity 8. Lewiston, N.Y.: Edwin Mellen, 1986.

Patterson, Stephen J. *The God of Jesus: The Historical Jesus and the Search for Meaning*. Harrisburg, Pa.: Trinity Press International, 1998.

Reed, Jonathan L. *Archaeology and the Galilean Jesus: A Re-Examination of the Evidence*. Harrisburg, Pa.: Trinity Press International, 2000.

Robinson, James M. *A New Quest of the Historical Jesus*. SBT 1/25. Naperville, Ill.: Allenson, 1959.

Sanders, E. P. *The Historical Figure of Jesus*. London: Penguin, 1993.

———. *Jesus and Judaism*. Philadelphia: Fortress Press, 1985.

Schweitzer, Albert. *The Quest of the Historical Jesus*. 1st Complete Edition. Edited by John Bowden. Translated by W. Montgomery, J. R. Coates, Susan Cupitt, and John Bowden. Minneapolis: Fortress Press, 2001.

Theissen, Gerd, and Annette Merz. *The Historical Jesus: A Comprehensive Guide*. Translated by John Bowden. Minneapolis: Fortress Press, 1999.

Vermes, Geza. *The Changing Faces of Jesus*. London: Allen Lane, 2000.

———. *Jesus the Jew: A Historian's Reading of the Gospels*. Minneapolis: Fortress Press, 1981.

Wright, N. T. *Jesus and the Victory of God*. Christian Origins and the Question of God 2. Minneapolis: Fortress Press, 1996.

SELECT BIBLIOGRAPHY ON PARABLES

Bailey, Kenneth E. *Poet and Peasant: A Literary-Cultural Approach to the Parables in Luke*. Grand Rapids: Eerdmans, 1976.

———. *Through Peasant Eyes: More Lucan Parables, Their Culture and Style*. Grand Rapids: Eerdmans, 1980.

Carlston, Charles E. *The Parables of the Triple Tradition*. Philadelphia: Fortress Press, 1975.

Carter, Warren, and John Paul Heil. *Matthew's Parables: Audience-oriented Perspectives*. CBQMS 30. Washington, D.C.: Catholic Biblical Association, 1998.

Crossan, John Dominic. *Cliffs of Fall: Paradox and Polyvalence in the Parables of Jesus*. New York: Crossroad, 1980.

———. *In Parables: The Challenge of the Historical Jesus*. New York: Harper & Row, 1973.

———. "The Parables of Jesus." *Int* 56 (2002) 247–59.

Dodd, C. H. *The Parables of the Kingdom*. Rev. ed. New York: Scribners, 1961.

Donahue, John R. *The Gospel in Parable: Metaphor, Narrative and Theology in the Synoptic Gospels*. Philadelphia: Fortress Press, 1988.

Elliott, John H. "Matthew 20:1-15: A Parable of Invidious Comparison and Evil Eye Accusation." *BTB* 22 (1992) 52–65.

Gowler, David B. *What Are They Saying about the Parables?* New York: Paulist, 2000.

Herzog, William R. II. *Parables as Subversive Speech: Jesus as Pedagogue of the Oppressed*. Louisville: Westminster John Knox, 1994.

Jeremias, Joachim. *The Parables of Jesus*. Translated by S. H. Hooke. 2nd ed. New York: Scribners, 1972.

Oakman, Douglas E. "Was Jesus a Peasant? Implications for Reading the Samaritan Story (Luke 10:30-35)." *BTB* 22 (1992) 117–25.

Rohrbaugh, Richard L. "The Parable of the Talents/Pounds: A Text of Terror?" *BTB* 23 (1993) 32–39.

Scott, Bernard Brandon. *Hear Then the Parable: A Commentary on the Parables of Jesus*. 2nd ed. Minneapolis: Fortress Press, forthcoming.

———. *Jesus: Symbol-maker for the Kingdom*. Philadelphia: Fortress Press, 1981.

Via, Dan O. Jr. *The Parables: Their Literary and Existential Dimension*. Philadelphia: Fortress Press, 1967.

Wilder, Amos N. *Jesus' Parables and the War of Myths: Essays on Imagination in the Scripture*. Edited by James Breech. Philadelphia: Fortress Press, 1982.

SELECT BIBLIOGRAPHY ON THE GOSPEL OF MARK

Achtemeier, Paul J. "Mark, Gospel of." In *ABD* 4:541–57.

———. "Miracles and the Historical Jesus: A Study of Mark 9:14-29." *CBQ* 37 (1975) 471–91.

———. "The Origin and Function of the Pre-Markan Miracle Catenae." *JBL* 91 (1972) 198–221.

———. "Toward the Isolation of Pre-Markan Miracle Catenae." *JBL* 89 (1970) 265–91.

Aichele, George. *Jesus Framed*. BibLim. London: Routledge, 1996.

Anderson, Janice Capel, and Stephen D. Moore, eds. *Mark and Method: New Approaches in Biblical Studies*. Minneapolis: Fortress Press, 1992.

Best, Ernest. *Disciples and Discipleship: Studies in the Gospel according to Mark*. Edinburgh: T. & T. Clark, 1986.

Black, C. Clifton. *The Disciples according to Mark: Markan Redaction in Current Debate*. JSNTSup 27. Sheffield: JSOT Press, 1989.

———. *Mark: Images of an Apostolic Interpreter.* SPNT. Minneapolis: Fortress Press, 2000.

Collins, Adela Yarbro. *The Beginning of the Gospel: Probings of Mark in Context.* Minneapolis: Fortress Press, 1992.

Donahue, John R. *The Gospel in Parable: Metaphor, Narrative, and Theology in the Synoptic Gospels.* Philadelphia: Fortress Press, 1988.

———, and Daniel J. Harrington. *The Gospel of Mark.* SacPag 2. Collegeville, Minn.: Liturgical, 2002.

Fowler, Robert M. *Let the Reader Understand: Reader-Response Criticism and the Gospel of Mark.* Minneapolis: Fortress Press, 1991.

Juel, Donald H. *The Gospel of Mark.* IBT. Nashville: Abingdon, 1999.

———. *A Master of Surprise: Mark Interpreted.* Minneapolis: Fortress Press, 1994.

Kelber, Werner H. *Mark's Story of Jesus.* Philadelphia: Fortress Press, 1979.

———, editor. *The Passion in Mark: Studies on Mark 14–16.* Philadelphia: Fortress Press, 1976.

Kermode, Frank. *The Genesis of Secrecy: On the Interpretation of Mark.* Cambridge: Harvard Univ. Press, 1979.

Kingsbury, Jack Dean. *The Christology of Mark.* Philadelphia: Fortress Press, 1980.

Mack, Burton L. *The Myth of Innocence: Mark and Christian Origins.* Philadelphia: Fortress Press, 1988.

Malbon, Elizabeth Struthers. *Narrative Space and Mythic Meaning in Mark.* NVBS. San Francisco: Harper & Row, 1986.

Malina, Bruce J., and Richard L. Rohrbaugh. *A Social-Scientific Commentary on the Synoptic Gospels.* 2nd ed. Minneapolis: Fortress Press, 2003.

Marxsen, Willi. *Mark the Evangelist.* Translated by James Boyce. Nashville: Abingdon, 1969.

Moloney, Francis J. *The Gospel of Mark: A Commentary.* Peabody, Mass.: Hendrickson, 2002.

Peterson, Dwight M. *The Origins of Mark: The Markan Community in Current Debate.* BibIntSer 48. Leiden: Brill, 2000.

Rhoads, David, Donald Michie, and Joanna Dewey. *Mark as Story: An Introduction to the Narrative of the Gospel.* 2nd ed. Minneapolis: Fortress Press, 1999.

Robbins, Vernon K. *Jesus the Teacher: A Socio-Rhetorical Interpretation of Mark.* Philadelphia: Fortress Press, 1984.

Robinson, James M. *The Problem of History in Mark and Other Marcan Studies.* Philadelphia: Fortress Press, 1982.

Rohrbaugh, Richard L. "The Social Location of the Markan Audience." *Int* 47 (1993) 380–95.

Telford, William, editor. *The Interpretation of Mark.* IRT 7. Philadelphia: Fortress Press, 1985.

Tolbert, Mary Ann. *Sowing the Gospel: Mark's World in Literary-Historical Perspective.* Minneapolis: Fortress Press, 1989.

Via, Dan O. *The Ethics of Mark's Gospel—In the Middle of Time.* Philadelphia: Fortress, 1985.

———. *Kerygma and Comedy in the New Testament: A Structuralist Approach to Hermeneutic.* Philadelphia: Fortress Press, 1975.

Weeden, Theodore J. *Mark—Traditions in Conflict.* Philadelphia: Fortress Press, 1971.

Select Bibliography on New Testament Theology

Adam, A. K. M. *Making Sense of New Testament Theology: "Modern" Problems and Prospects.* SABH 11. Macon, Ga.: Mercer Univ. Press, 1995.

Balla, Peter. *Challenges to New Testament Theology: An Attempt to Justify the Enterprise.* WUNT 2/95. Tübingen: Mohr/Siebeck, 1997.

Boers, Hendrikus. *What Is New Testament Theology? The Rise of Criticism and the Problem of a Theology of the New Testament.* GBS. Minneapolis: Fortress Press, 1979.

Braun, Herbert. "The Problem of a Theology of the New Testament." *JTC* 1 (1965) 169–83.

Bultmann, Rudolf. *Theology of the New Testament.* Translated by Kendrick Grobel. 2 vols. New York: Scribners, 1951–55. [German ed. 1948–51]

Caird, G. B. *New Testament Theology.* Edited and completed by L. D. Hurst. Oxford: Clarendon, 1994.

Childs, Brevard S. *Biblical Theology of the Old and New Testaments.* Minneapolis: Fortress Press, 1995.

Conzelmann, Hans. *An Outline of the Theology of the New Testament.* London: SCM, 1969. [German ed. 1968]

Dunn, James D. G. *Unity and Diversity in the New Testament: An Inquiry into the Character of Earliest Christianity.* 2nd ed. Philadelphia: Trinity, 1990.

Fuller, Reginald H. "New Testament Theology." In *The New Testament and Its Modern Interpreters,* edited by Eldon J. Epp and George W. MacRae, 565–84. Philadelphia: Fortress Press, 1989.

Goppelt, Leonhard. *Theology of the New Testament.* Translated by John E. Alsup. Grand Rapids: Eerdmans, 1981–82. [German ed. 1975–76]

Hasel, Gerhard F. *New Testament Theology: Basic Issues in the Current Debate.* Grand Rapids: Eerdmans, 1978.

Jeremias, Joachim. *New Testament Theology.* vol. 1: *The Proclamation of Jesus.* Translated by John Bowden. New York: Scribners, 1971. [German ed. 1971]

Käsemann, Ernst. "The Problem of a New Testament Theology." *NTS* 19 (1973) 235–45.

Kümmel, Werner Georg. *Theology of the New Testament according to Its Major Witnesses: Jesus–Paul–John.* Translated by John Steeley. Nashville: Abingdon, 1973.

Morgan, Robert C. *The Nature of New Testament Theology: The Contributions of William Wrede and Adolf Schlatter.* SBT 2/25. Naperville, Ill.: Allenson, 1973.

———. "Theology, New Testament." In *ABD* 6.473–83.

Robinson, James M. "The Future of New Testament Theology." *Religious Studies Review* 2 (1976) 17–23.

Schmithals, Walter. *The Theology of the First Christians.* Translated by O. C. Dean Jr. Louisville: Westminster John Knox, 1997. [German ed. 1994]

Schnackenburg, Rudolf. *New Testament Theology Today.* New York: Herder & Herder, 1963. [French ed. 1961]

Strecker, Georg. *Theology of the New Testament.* Translated by M. Eugene Boring. Louisville: Westminster John Knox, 2000.

Thompson, Marianne Meye. *The Promise of the Father: Jesus and God in the New Testament.* Louisville: Westminster John Knox, 2000.

Via, Dan O. *What Is New Testament Theology?* GBS. Minneapolis: Fortress Press, 2002.

Index of Modern Authors

Editor's Note: Dates have been supplied for authors of earlier generations in order to provide historical context.

Index of Terms and Phrases

149

Index of Ancient Sources

FORTRESS CLASSICS
— *in* —
BIBLICAL STUDIES

EDITED BY K. C. HANSON

The Quest of the Historical Jesus
First Complete Edition
Albert Schweitzer
Edited by John Bowden

Water for a Thirsty Land
Israelite Literature and Religion
Hermann Gunkel

Jesus and the Message of the New Testament
Joachim Jeremias

The Spirit and the Word
Prophecy and Tradition in Ancient Israel
Sigmund Mowinckel

Parable and Gospel
Norman Perrin

The Fiery Throne
The Prophets and Old Testament Theology
Walther Zimmerli

CPSIA information can be obtained at www.ICGtesting.com
Printed in the USA
269346BV00001B/1/A